Blanche

Her Life, Her Kids, Her Food

Created by

Mary Van Kempen Nilsen

and Her Siblings

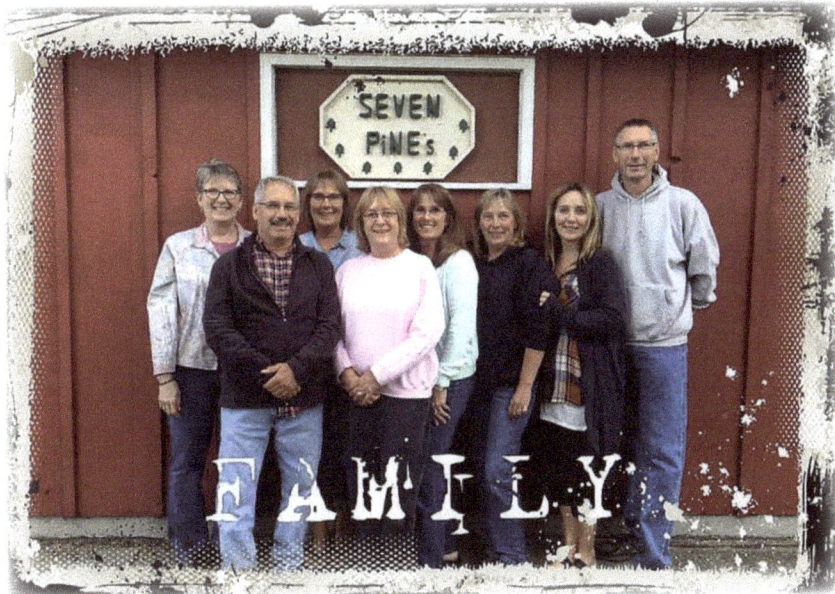

ISBN: 978-0-9998819-2-7

Copies of this book can be ordered online.

Designed by:

Mary Ylvisaker Nilsen of

ZION PUBLISHING SERVICES

Des Moines, Iowa
www.zionpublishing.org

Printed in the USA

This book is dedicated to our 91-year-old mother, grandmother, and great grandmother, Blanche Van Kempen

on the spot
with Chris Shaffer

Happy 90th Birthday!
Blanche

The little gray house at 7 Pine Street

Foreword

"It's the little gray house at the bottom of the hill—the one by the Green River." Such location descriptions were common place in a community where the activities of the day centered around landmarks like "the dam" or "Quik Stop," "the bowling alley" or games on Pine Street: "Seven Steps Around the House," "Ante I Over," "kick the Can," and "Captain, May I"?

Of course, what such descriptions never fully grasp is the humanity connected to those landmark locations. But for those who have been fortunate enough to step inside "the little gray house at the bottom of the hill—the one by the Green River," an immediate recognition takes place. This is not just any location. Not just a house. It is a home—warm and inviting, small in size, enormous in hospitality, filled with the voices of a family and the aroma of food, led by a matriarch, though she is much too humble to see herself that way, named Blanche.

And here's what is true for many: Innumerable cups of coffee and attention to our individual tastes. Use of garden fresh vegetables. Spam to stretch a meal. The ubiquitous hot dish. And a willingness to expend most of what she had for any celebration. This has forever left a mark in our hearts, a mark that has helped to guide our journeys, the kind of respite we can only hope to pass along to our own family—our children and descendants yet to come, our friends present and those yet to be: a landmark to guide their journeys.

The prayer for this book is a simple one: That the atmosphere, the aroma, the hospitality found in "the little gray house at the bottom of the hill, the one by the Green River" might fill your home, leaving a mark in the hearts of all who enter.

Give her the fruit of her hands,
And let her works praise
Her at the gates.
Proverbs 31:31

Introduction

*"Her children rise up and bless her"**

What better way to bless our mother, Blanche Van Kempen, than to gather together all her recipes, the inspiration for the food she prepared for decades as she fed the hungry mouths gathered around her table. This group of diners swelled to eleven. Then, through sickness, a car accident, and the natural moving out of grown children, Mother, now, cooks for one and looks forward to celebrating when we come to visit. What better way is there to enable her descendants to come to know their matriarch than through pictures and recipes and to be inspired by her own words. What better way to honor a life lived joyfully serving others.

While spearheaded by Blanche's youngest daughter, Mary Nilsen, all of us children have contributed pictures, recipes, and ideas for this tribute to our still vibrant 91-year-old mother.

Mom could have grown frustrated when the family outgrew their small home and there was, literally, no place for them to all sit down and eat. She could have given up when her beloved husband died of a fast growing cancer when the youngest of nine was only four years old. She could have fallen into despair when her precious son, Tom, 21, was killed in a car accident or when others of her children acted out in ways that worried her, or when a dear grandchild died or when her oldest daughter died. But she didn't!

Mom, for your courage, your stick-to-it-iveness, your hospitality, your life-long joy in feeding both the body and soul of everyone you love, we share these pictures and recipes with your loved ones—a way of keeping you close and giving us strength for the day and hope for the future.

With love and deepest gratitude from your children.

*Proverbs 31:28, *Today's English Version*

Table of Contents

Picture Gallery

Mom's mother and father's wedding

Dad's mother and father's wedding

James Van Kempen

James E. Van Kempen USN - PHM2
WWII - 1943-47   Korean War - 1950-5?

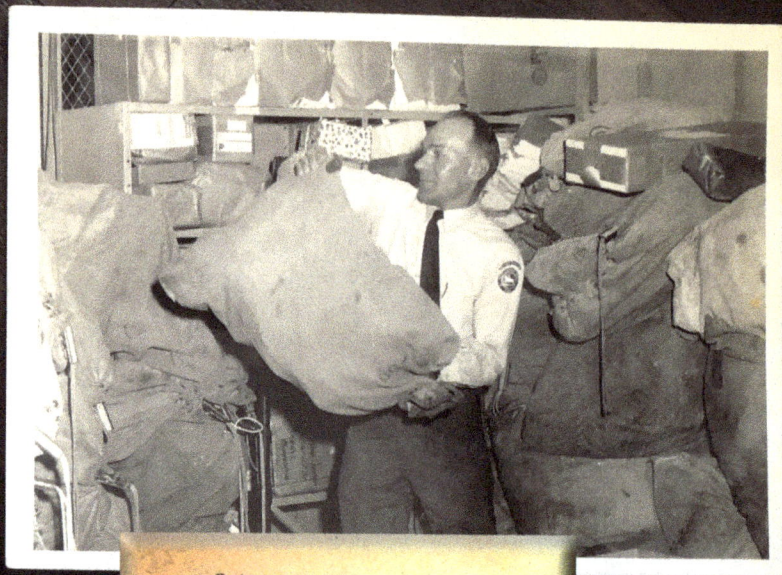

329-51-44
James Van Hengen P.h. m ?
Special augmented Hospital ...
U.S. Navy.

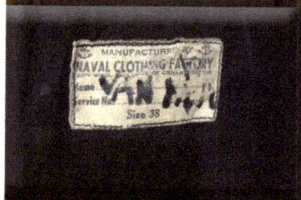

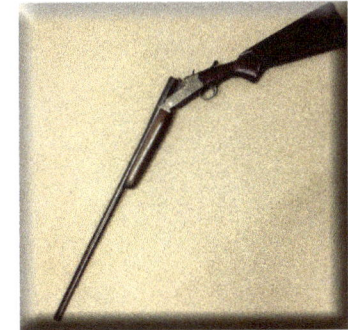

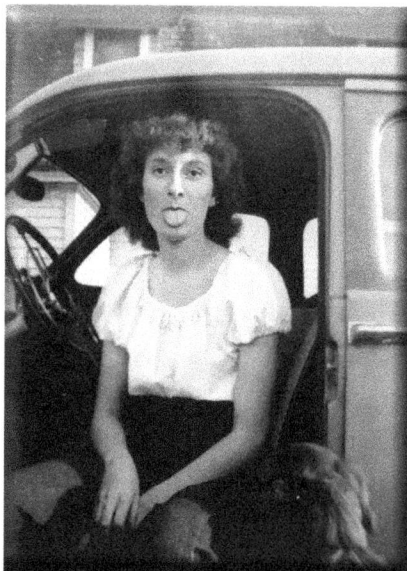

Blanche, daughter of Alfred & Kunda Gunda (Bertamus) Bresson, was born September 20, 1928, in Canby, Minnesota. Blanche attended Yellow Medicine Country School through the 4th grade, before moving with her family to Morris in 1937, where she attended country school until the 8th grade. She graduated from Morris High School in 1946.

Wedding Guests
and Gifts

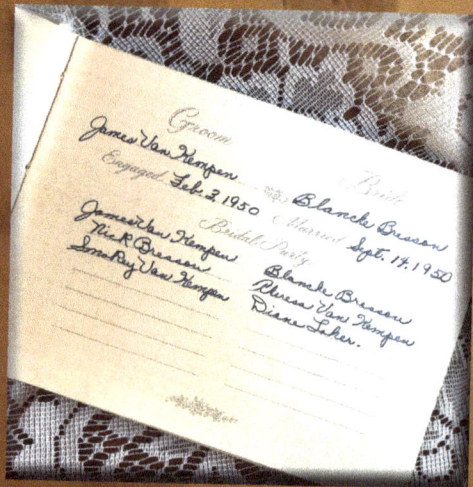

Van Kempen - Bresson

The Assumption church in Morris was the scene of the marriage of Miss Blanche Bresson, daughter of Mr. and Mrs. A. D. Bresson of Morris, and James Van Kempen, son of Mr. and Mrs. Hubert

Photo by Bakey

Van Kempen, of Morris. The wedding was solemnized at 9:30 o'clock Thursday morning, September 14. Rev. Father Raymond Jacques performing the double ring ceremony.

"The Wedding March" by Gulmant was played by Sister Alicia. She was accompanied by the junior choir which sang. "Ava Maria." "Jesu Mitis," "Jesus, Jesus Come to Me," and "Panis Angelicus."

The bride, given in marriage by her father, wore a gown of heavy white satin styled with a long train with a fitted bodice. The neckline was of net trimmed with lace. The long sleeve came to points over the hands. Her white fingertip veil was edged in lace with a crown of pearls and lace. Her jewelry was a wrist watch from the groom Her flowers were a bouquet of red roses

Attending the bride as bridesmaid was Miss Theresa Van Kempen, sister of the groom. Her gown was of lavender frosted organdy, fashioned somewhat like the bride's except she had short sleeves. She wore white short gloves and a wreath of white and yellow asters for a crown. Her flowers were yellow glads and white asters. Her gift from the bride was gold earrings.

The flower girl was Diane Loher, niece of the bride. She wore a pale green frosted organdy dress which was fashioned of white and yellow asters for a crown and white gloves. She carried a lace basket of Colonial flowers.

Nick Bresson of Morris, brother of the bride, was best man. His gift from the groom was a key chain. The groom and best man and the ringbearer wore white dinner jackets. Their boutonnieres were red roses. The ushers were Charles Rudnicki, friend of the groom, and Henry Schmidt, Jr., cousin of the groom. Their gifts from the groom were necktie clasps. The ringbearer was Smokey Van Kempen, nephew of the groom. He carried the rings on a white satin pillow.

A dinner attended by 65 guests was given in the church parlors. The table was centered with a three-tier wedding cake decorated in lavender and green. The waitresses were the Misses Alice Bengston, Belva Niss and Carol Stephens, and Mrs. Wayne Sprouls.

On their wedding trip the couple went to Wyoming and Montana. They are now at home at 402 Nevada avenue in this city.

The bride, a lifelong resident of the community, is a graduate of Morris high school. She is employed as a dental assistant in the office of Dr. O. T. Johnson

The groom is also a lifelong resident of the community. He attended the West Central school and served for four years in the United States Navy. He is now employed with the H. J. Lohge

Dad

After Blanche graduated from high school, she was employed at Dr. Johnson/Dr. Vanderhoof Dental office in Morris and at the Four Seasons Country Club. She married James E. Van Kempen on September 14th, 1950, at Assumption Catholic Church in Morris, Minn., by Monsignor Fearon. Jim and Blanche continued to live in Morris until Jim was called back by the Naval Reserves for the Korean War. They moved to Memphis, Tenn., for two years and then settling back in Morris. They enjoyed playing cards and dancing. Every spring they also planted a large vegetable garden which they enjoyed tending to, weeding, and harvesting together.

Mom

Blanche's Breakfast Bakes

Egg, Sausage Bake   9 X 13.
                       350° 45

Cut off 3-4 crust on bread - Butter
Cover with Sausage or ham or.
chop chen_
Then shredded cheese
Make_
  6 eggs_ 2 cups half & half or milk
       salt/pepper_ Pour over
Bread & etc - cook or let stand over nite

Judy - Egg Bake - grease pan
14 slices bread   9 X 13 - 350° 1 hr.

7 slices broke up on bottom
2 cups ham diced
1 - 8 oz swiss cheese
1 - 8 oz cheddar cheese
Mix 6 eggs - 3 cups milk 1 teas.
        ½ teas - onion salt - dry mustard
tear 7 more slices Then pour
milk - egg mix over that. (over)

Can make nite B/4 or in A. M.
In the A.M - crush 3 cups
Frosted Flakes cereal - put on top -
Drizzle ½ cup ole over.
Bake uncovered - If refr. - take
out let stand for ½ hr -

Recipe for: _Egg & such –_
from the kitchen of: _8 X 8 glass pan –_

Make scrambled eggs
& Jimmy Dean sussig –
Take the skin off & Break
up & put in scrambled eggs –
¼ chopped onion salt &
¼ c gr. pepper. Pepper.
Mix all these with
unscrambled eggs   serves: ____

Bake 30-45 min in 300
oven. Serve with toast.

Sunday Brunch – grease 9×13 – 350°
1 hr.

3 cups seasoned croutons
1 Stick ole
2 cups milk
1 lb. fried crumbled Bacon
2 cups shredded cheese
1 can Mushroom Soup
10 eggs.
Over Croutons on the bottom
Sprinkle with Cheese & Bacon.

Beat remaining & pour into pan.
Cover with foil & Bake uncovered
1 hr. Let stand 5-10
min B/4 cutting –

Blue Berry Egg Bake -

1 loaf cubed Master Muffin cut up -
Put half in 9 x 13 pan -
2 pkg cream cheese
1 cup Blue Berries (fresh or (frozen))
12 lge eggs -
1/3 cup maple syrup.
2 cups milk

Sauce ;   Put all together & cook
    1 cup Sugar 2 tbsp cornstarch

1 cup water -̶t̶o̶g̶e̶t̶h̶e̶r̶-
1 cup Blueberries - 2 tbsp ole
Mix together sugar, cornstarch & water -
cook over medium high heat - stirring
constantly until thick, sprinkle phie over
Bread - add some Blueberries - add rest of cubes
whisk eggs - syrup / milk - Pour over & chill
overnite - Cover with sauce - oven 365
for 35 min - Remove foil & bake for 35 min -
more - let set for a lil bit

25

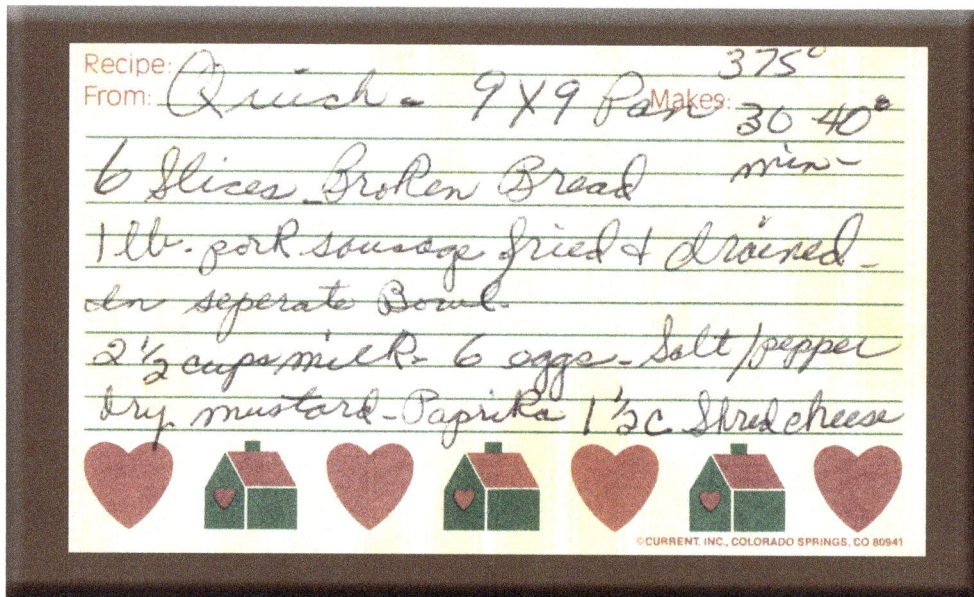

Recipe:
From: Quiche - 9 X 9 Pan

Makes: 375°
30 40° min~

6 Slices Broken Bread

1 lb. pork sausage fried & drained -
in seperate Bowl -

2 ½ cups milk - 6 eggs - Salt / pepper

dry mustard - Paprika 1 ½ c. Shred cheese

©CURRENT, INC., COLORADO SPRINGS, CO 80941

🌱 26

Breakfast Casserole   9 X 13 – 350° 1½ hr. greased

2 ½ c herbal croutons
2 cups cheddar cheese (grated)
2 pkge Sausage – Brown & drain
8 eggs
¾ tsp – dry Mustard
2 cups milk
1 can celery soup
½ c milk

(over)

Spread croutons in 9 X 13 (not glass)
top with cheese & sausage
cover & put in frig over nite.
Next A.M. Mix Soup – Milk & pour over
casserole – Cook 1½ hr. Cut & serve
in squares –

Impossible Quich
Crumble 12-14 slices fried bacon
or chopped ham or Spam.
   5-6 eggs. salt & pepper.
1/4 c. green pepper
1 cup shredded cheese
1/3 c onion chopped fine
   2 cups milk
1/2 c biscuit mix
Put in greased 9x9 - Put Bacon
or ham or Spam & cheese. onion - gr. pepper
on the bottom. Beat eggs - milk &
1/2 c. biscuit together - Pour on top
   350° 50 min - Let stand 4 5 min
B/4 cutting

Delicious - Ctry Style Eggs -
Make completely in Micro Wave
1 lb - fried - drained - crumbled Bacon
2 tbls ole - ½ C chopped onion - ½ C, cut gr -
pepper - 5 or 6 hash Br. sq. Put these
4 ingred - in bottom of pie plate - Hash
Browns first - Melt ole & pour over top w/
onions & gr. pepper - Put in Micro 6 min -
Mix 6 eggs - ⅓ C milk - ½ teas salt &
Pepper - Pour over hash Br. mix & cook on
hi 3 min - Stir & cook 3 more min -
Then add 1 ½ C - Shredded cheddar cheese -
& Bacon - Micro wave 1 more min -
Let Stand 5 min o
Ive made it in a 8 X 8 cake dish
also - Just cover whole bottom with
H. B. Sorta like a brunch.
Dan made this when I was their.
If left over - Just Micro Wave
     pieces o

Cinnamon Rolls   9 X 13 - 350° -
                              20 min.

Cover sides & bottom of sheet pan
with mixture of
   1 c. Br. Sugar -
   1 stick ole
   2 tbls - of milk or ½ & ½ -   ↑ don't
   1 small butterscotch pudding -   use all
Raise & bake - When done remove
from oven - Cool Slightly & turn pan
upside down onto a sheet.

~ Do we ever tell our kids how she walked everywhere she went for years because we didn't own a car, and she didn't know how to drive even after we did get a car?

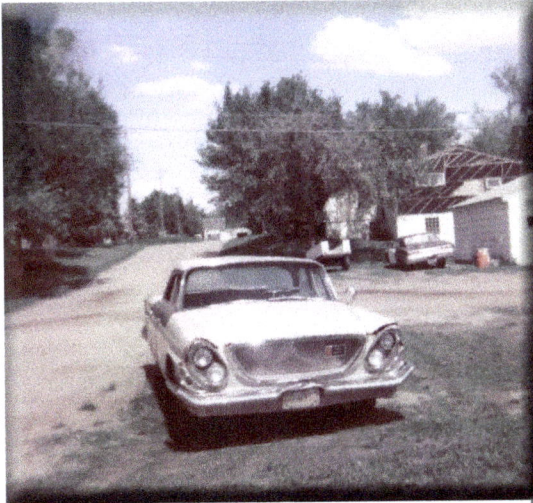

Frozen Bread Caramel rolls

2 loaves frozen Bread
½ cup ole - melted
1 cup Br. Sugar
1 pkg. Butter Scotch not instant
or vanilla - small pkg
1 teas cinnamon
1 tbls. milk ⎫ liquid

grease 9 X 13 = let Bread almost
thaw then break up 1 loaf all
over pan - Pour over this - Then
break 2nd loaf on top - Let set 3 hrs.
Bake 350 - 25 to 30 - min -
Let set 15 min when you take it out -
(over)

Bake after 3 hrs at 350° -
About 25 min - Cool 15 min
B/4 turning over the pan -
Delicious -

Nikki

31

Recipe:
From: Apple Cinnamon French Toast   Makes:

5 Tbls. ole - 4 or 5 apples peeled - sliced in melted ole & stir & cook till done -

1 c dk. or lite Br. Sugar
                                    1 teas cinnamon
2 Tbls. dark corn syrup
8 slices - French Bread -   (over)

©CURRENT, INC., COLORADO SPRINGS, CO 80941

3 lge eggs - 1 c milk 1 teas vanilla,
After apples are sauted in ole a
little bit - add Br. Sugar - syrup & cinnamon
to apples - Stir till Br. Sugar is desolved -
Put in 9 X 13 pan - Put French Bread over
that - In bowl mix eggs - milk & vanilla
Mix well - pour over bread - cover with
saran + refrigerate over nite.
Next A.M. heat oven 350° - 375° - 30-35 min.
Cool in pan 5 min. If you want tip over on
tray - Spoon apples evenly over Breads -

Patte Caramel Rolls-

① thaw- 2 loaves frozen Bread in refrig overnight-

② Take one loaf & tear into pieces & lay in bottom ungreased 9 X 13 pan

③ Mix together ½ cup ole - 1c Br. Sugar - 2 tbls. milk / lge. vanilla Pudding (not Instant) - ~~cinnamon~~

④ Spread over 1st mixture of Bread-

⑤ Sprinkle with cinnmon.

⑥ tear 2nd loaf & lay over caramel mixture.

Let rise 2 hrs.

Bake at 350° for 30 min.

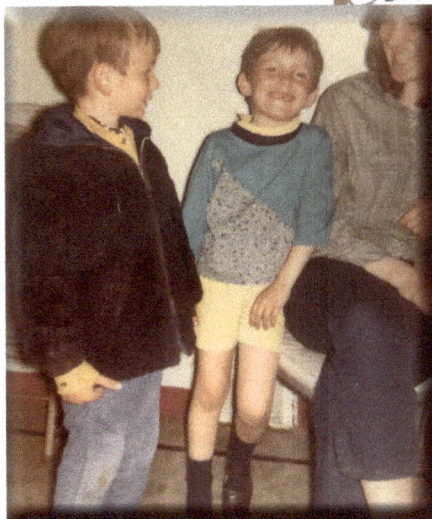

33 🌿

Easy Ham/Egg Bake or Fried Bacon Bits
x9 - 350° -   instead of eggs -
Make nite B/4 or in A. M.
4 slices cubed Bread -
1 cup - shred cheese -
1 cup - cubed ham -
Mix & pour over - 1½ C milk
Bake - 1 hr. or a little) 4 eggs -
less - I doubled it one day) 1 teas - dry mustard
so can easily be) a little less than ¼ cup
done - flour -

Overnite Caramel Rolls (Easy)

Set one frozen loaf out to thaw a little (about 1 hr. or less). Just so you can cut easily. Butter bottom & sides of Bundt Pan. If you want chop & sprinkle nuts on top of butter -
Cut pieces about ½" thick. Put wedges in buttered (use ole) pan. Squeeze them in so they all fit. Sprinkle ½ pkg of butterscotch pudding on dough. Melt.
¾ c Br. Sugar - ½ c ole - 1 teas, cinnamon -
Pour over rolls - leave on ctr. overnite,
In the A.M bake at 350° - 20-25 min.
Let set in pan 10 min - B/4 turning onto the plate -
    Put plate on top of Bundt pan &
flip quickly -

Our home at 7 Pine, Morris, Minnesota

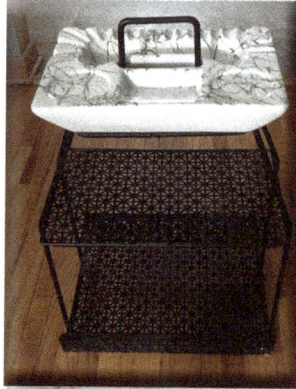

Blanche's Hot Dishes

Spinach & Ham La Sagna
30 min -

6 - Lasagna noodles (4 ozs.)
1 - 10 oz pkge. frozen chopped Spinach
2 cups skim milk
2 tbls, dried minced onion
1½ c. diced ham
½ teas - Italian seasoning (crushed)
1 cup low fat cottage cheese -
1 c - shredded mozzarella cheese -

Cook noodles for 10-12 min. Drain. Rinse
with cold water - drain again, Set aside &
cook spinach - according to pkge. drain well -
For the sauce combine milk, cornstarch &
onion - cook & stir till thickened/bubbly -
Cook & stir 2 min. more - Spread 2 tbls. of the
sauce evenly on the bottom of 10"X 6"X 2" baking
Dish. Stir ham & Italian seasoning into remain
sauce, 3 Lasagna noodles in Dish, Spread ⅓
sauce - Layer Spinach atop. Layer another ⅓ of
sauce, Cottage cheese & ½ mozzarella - Place

(Con't)
Spinach + Ham La Sagna - Place
remaining noodles atop. Top with remaining
sauce - mozzarella.

Bake - 375° oven for 30/35 min. or till
heated through. Let stand 10 min - 8/4
serving -

Recipe for: _Swedish Meatballs_
from the kitchen of: _____
1 lb. hamb.   1 tbls parsley
                               flakes
½ lb. ground pork   2 teas salt
½ c onion   1 teas. Worcestershi
¾ c. cracker or breadcrumbs
1 egg - ½ c milk.
mix all these & refrig - 2 hrs.
Then shape into Balls - about 50 &
size - fry in grease   serves: _____

Remove browned meat balls & then
add to grease of (¼ cup) ¼ c flour
1 teas paprika
½ salt - 2 cup or more water
    ¾ c sour cream - gradually
stir in sour cr, & then reboil 1 min
add meat balls - cook slow & low
for ½ hr - I freeze some of this
& the gravy. Makes 2 or 3 meals

Meatballs on Rice –

you used
to make
this

1 can tomato Soup
1 can onion Soup
2 tbls. cornstarch
3 tbls. Br. Sugar
1 tbls. worcester Shire
1/4 c vinegar.
Mix together – Then fry.
1 lb. hamb – 1/2 lb susage – 1 egg –
1/2 c cracker crumbs

Salt &
pepper

Serve
warm
dinner
rolls

(over)

Brown – put in gravy &
simmer – stirring gently.
Serve on rice –

41

Recipe: Farmhouse B-B-Que Muffins

From: _____ Makes: _____

1 tube (10 oz.) refrigated buttermilk
biscuts

1 lb. lean hamb.

1/2 c Retchup   Seperate dough into
3 tbls Brown Sugar   10 biscuts,
1 tbls. cider vinegar Flaten into 5" circles
1/2 teas chili powder Press each into a
1 cup shredded cheddar greased muffin
        cheese.   cup.

Set aside. Br. hamburger. Drain. In
bowl mix Retchup, Br. Sugar, vinegar &
chili powder. Stir & then add to meat &
mix well. Put mixture into biscut cups in
muffin tin. Sprinkle with cheese.
350-375 · 20 min.

        Cool 5 min.

Makes 10 Muffins

Salesbury Steak - 350° - 30 - 40 min.

	Gravy
1 lb. hamb -	2 tbls. flour
¼ pkge dry onion soup mix	1½ c water
¼ cups dry bread crumbs	¾ pkge. onion
¼ c. milk	soup mix
1 egg -	

Combine all ings. for patties. Stir well.
Shape & brown in skillet. add patties to
Drain. the pan - cover. Put in oven
30 - 35 min - I double & freeze

43

Pizza Burgers

1 can Spam - grind or smash -
1½ lbs. hamb - fried - drained
1 - pkg. grated cheese (2 cups -
1 tsp. Sage
2 - tsp oregano
¼ - tea. salt.
1½ or more Ragu or Prego -
Set in frig - even freeze - over

a pen face buns on cookie
sheet 350° 8 to 10 min.
Watch maybe less.
I butter halfs -

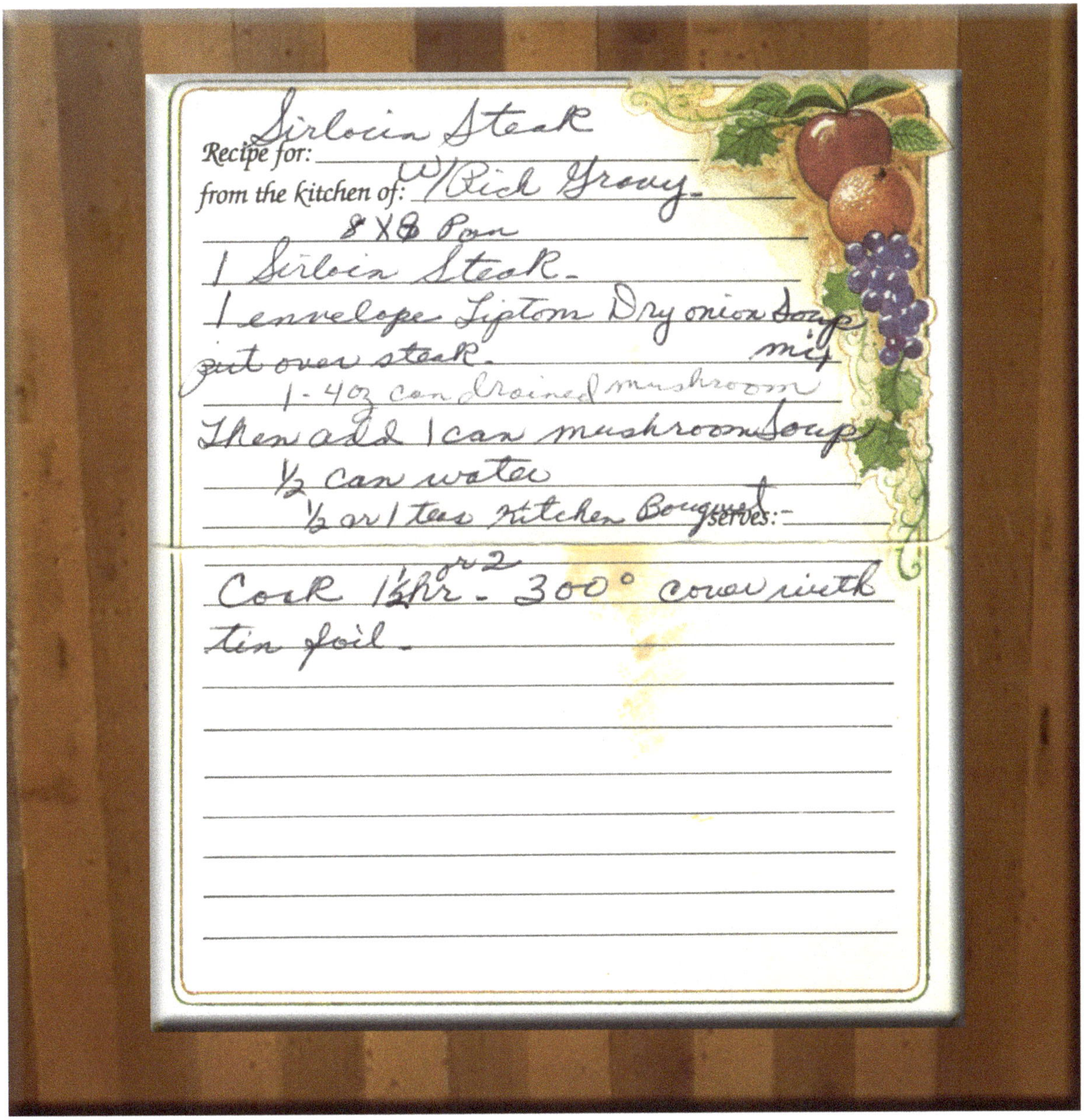

Recipe for: _Sirloin Steak_

from the kitchen of: _W/Rich Gravy_

8 X 8 Pan

1 Sirloin Steak

1 envelope Lipton Dry onion Soup mix
put over steak.

1 - 4 oz can drained mushroom

Then add 1 can mushroom Soup

½ can water

½ or 1 tea Kitchen Bouquet

serves: -

Cook 1½ hr or 2 - 300° cover with
tin foil.

Judys - Xmas Det Dish
Raw meat Balls   1½ hrs -
                        350 -
Pour over:
 1 chili sauce - 1 tbls. lemon
 2 cups sauer Kraut   juice
 1 - Jelly cranberries
 ¾ c. Br. Sugar
 2 tbls tomato juice

Pour over
raw meat
balls -

Garden Skillet Supper -
1 c uncooked long grain rice
1 tbls. oil - 2 garlic cloves - chopped
1 cup onion - ½ c green pepper ½ c red pepper
1 lb. gr. beef. Browned - drained -
2 cups chopped seeded tomatoes -
Cook rice as directed. Saute in oil garlic
onion & peppers - Stir in tomatoes - Beef &
rice -

Steak in a foil -
Piece of Steak -
1 pkge Dry Onion Soup -
1 can Campbell Soup -
jar mushrooms (drained) if you
                    want -
Cover with foil - Cook 1½ hr - 300°

Favorite Recipe for: Hamburger hot dish.
From the Kitchen of:

Brown 2 lbs hamb. onions & celery.
Add.
2 Boxes frozen mixed vegie broccoli
2 cans water chestnuts — Cut in half
1 can bamboo shoots.
2 cans chk rice soup
1 can cream of chen.
1 can cream celery
3-4 tbls. soy sauce   Makes:

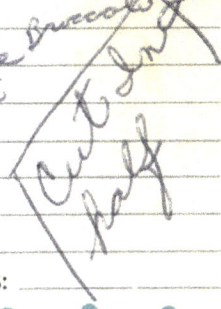

Spread 1 lge pk chow mein
Noodles on top -

47

Rueben Casserole 6-8- Servings

8 oz wide noodles cooked & drained
3 tbls ole -
1 can Sauerkraut (drained)
2 cups chopped corned beef
2 med tomatoes peeled & sliced -
1/4 C - Thousand Island dressing
2 cups Shredded Swiss cheese
1/2 teas. caraway seed.   [350° Grease
                                (Set aside)

Drain noodles - Put in bowl - Add oled
Coat - Layer all noodles - Sauerkraut, corned
beef - Then sliced tomatoes - Dot with
thousand Island dressing & then dot;
& sprinkle with cheese -
Top with caraway seed -
Bake covered - 350° - 40 min. Uncover
& Bake for 15 min - or until Bubbly -

SauerKraut hot dish —   8X8
                         9X13
                              salt-
Hamburger — fried — on bottom
celery —   onion + celery — ½ c onions
SauerKraut — 1 can juice + all

Thin noodles. 2 cups. broken up
         uncooked —
1) Mushroom Soup + ~~be with~~
1 celery Soup —   1 cup water
   last half hr sprinkle with
  cheese I use mixture of —
       Cheddar + mozarella
350-45 min. then add cheese
               for 15 min —

49

Hash Brown Hot Dish - 350° - 1 hr.

Big - 9 x 13 - & mix in larg bowl.
    Melt 1/3 cup ole
1 - 2 lb - bag hash browns
1 can potato soup
1 can celery soup
2 tbls. chopped onion
1 - 8 oz sour cream
1 tsp salt - little less
1/4 pepper Teas -

mix all together
Mix 1/3 cup melted
ole + 2 or more
cups Corn flakes.
Put over the top
(over)

1 cup Shredded cheese
1 1/2

I just sprinkled pepper - Sprinkle
. rest of shredded cheese - Then
I covered last 15 min. piece of tin
foil - Oh. yeah, Either plain - I
put 1 1/2 cups diced ham -

50

Crock Pot Dit Dish-
   7 hrs- on low-
   4 cken Breasts
   2 pkge Stuffing Mix - 1 pkg?
1 can Cream of cken Soup
1 cup Sour cream   } together
1 cup water
Pour over 2 top items then add
Frozen green Strong Beans
   If you want 4 hrs. on high

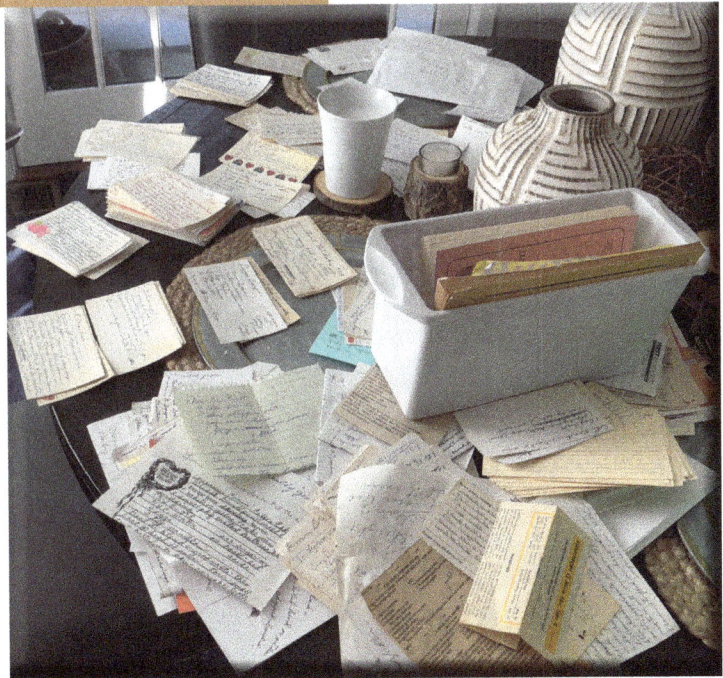

Hot dish - Simple . Easy & good.
1 lb. fried Lamb - or more -
6 c - raw potatoes
1 c - cooked & cut up carrots
1 c peas -
#1 - onion diced -
1 - Mushroom Soup) no water or
1 - celery Soup -) milk
Bake - slowly till done -
& cook carrots on top of stove for 15 mn.

cause they never seem to get done
in hot dishes -
made mistake of adding ½ c milk to
Soups & it was terrible soupy so dont
o that -

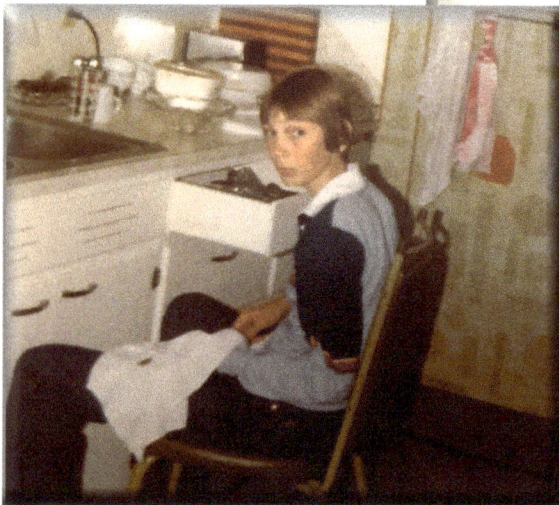

Recipe: One dish Chen/Rice Bake-
From: _____ Makes: _____

1 can Mushroom Soup
1 cup water
3/4 c uncooked rice long or regular
1/4 tsp. each paprika/pepper
4 skinless-boneless chen breast halves
① Heat oven 375°. ② 2 qt. shallow

baking dish. Mix soup-water-rice-
paprika & pepper. Place chen on rice mix
ture, Sprinkle with additional paprika &
pepper. ③ Cover-Bake for 45 min or
until done. Serve,

©CURRENT, INC.

Judy's

Recipe for: turkey or chicken

from the kitchen of: Sandwich - 9 X 13
    325° - 1 hr. 10 min.
                                    grease
12 slices bread
1/2 c. ole. & 2 teas. mustard - mix these
                                    2 & spread
1 c. cheddar cheese   on one side of
                                    bread.
1 c. peas . 2 tbs. pimento
2 c. turkey   or sm. jar
1/4 c onion

Then mix 4 eggs beaten serves: _____

1 can mushroom soup
1 1/2 c. milk - Pour over top
    very carefully - let soak
    in.

First 6 slices on bottom then
turkey - then shredded cheese & peas
mixture - Then other 6 bread.
Then pour liquid junk.
Grease pan.

Swt & Sour Ribs

Recipe for: _____

from the kitchen of: _____

3 lbs. ctry style ribs (lean)
½ c onion chopped
1 (8oz) tomato sauce
1 Tbls. Worcestershire Sauce
1 (#2) tidbits pineapple + juice
Salt & Pepper
¼ c gr. pepper
⅓ c vinegar   serves: _____
¼ c. Br. sugar
½ teas - dry mustard

Sprinkle ribs with salt & pepper & bake
1¼ hrs at 350° - Drain fat - while ribs
are baking, mix other "ingred. Together
& let stand. Then put sauce over
ribs & bake 1 hr. more at 350° -
Baste frequently with sauce
during baking.

55

Recipe: Creamy Chen / vegetables

From: _____ Makes: _____

4 Skinless Chen breasts -
1/8 tsp. garlic powder
1 can mushroom Soup.
1/2 c milk
1 tbsp - lemon juice.
1/4 tsp. crushed basil leaves
1 bag frozen vegie - broccoli cauliflower &
carrots.

(over)

Sprinkle Chen with garlic powder
Grease pan (skillet) & fry & brown chen -
Then set aside -
Add soup - milk - lemon juice - basil &
vegie. Heat to a boil. Return chen to pan
Cover & 350° or 300 - for 1/2 hr.

Recipe: Delicious Chen Hot dish -
From: _____ Makes: _____

Cook 6 chen Breasts - cool enuf to
handle + cut in pieces - put in a
greased 9X13 Pan -
In a bowl put 2 cans cream of Chen
Soup + 1 pt. Sour cream, Mix well -
Pour on top of chicken. Crush one roll
of Ritz crackers - Sprinkle over top -
then melt 2 sticks of oleo or butter &

Drizzle over top of crackers - then
sprinkle 3 or 2 teas poppy seed -
cook uncovered in oven - 350° 30-40 min

Serve over rice or as is.

Saucy Chen & Asparagus.

2 lbs. Asparagus Spears - halved.
4 to 6 pieces of skinless chen breasts
2 tbls. oil - fry - chen in -
½ teas. salt.   ¼ teas pepper
1 can cr. of chen soup -
½ cup mayo - 1 teas. lemon juice
½ teas - curry powder.
1 cup shredded cheddar cheese   (over)

If desired - partially cook asparagus. drain
Put in 9×9 greased pan - Brown chen in the
2 tbls. oil. Place asparagus in pan then
arrange browned chen over that. Season.
In a bowl - mix soup - mayo - lemon juice
& curry powder - Pour over chen. Covered
bake 350. 40 or 45 min. Sprinkle with
cheese. Let stand 5 min. B/4 serving.

Fry & Bake Chken

Chken Breasts -2-3
1 cup flour
2 teas salt / pepper
2 - teas - paprika
Put dry ing. in bag
& Chken & shake until
coated. Brown in ole.
Put in baking dish
Cover with:
½ cup honey
½ cup [?]

Recipe: Pork / Sauerkraut Supper -
From: _____ Makes: _____

1 - 16 oz - Irish potatoes (sliced. Drain
1 - 14 oz Sauerkraut - (Drained & rinsed)
1 apple chopped   4 Smoked
                          pork loin chops
1 tbls. Dijon mustard
½ c Apple juice   12 X 7 pan 350° 1
                          covered

Patoes in ungreased pan - Stir
Sauerkraut, apple & mustard tog
Then pour over potatoes with j
& Pork on top.

Slow Cooker Stuffing
in Crock pot

1 c. butter melted
2 c. chopped celery
1 c. " " onion
1 teas poultry seasoning
1½ tsp sage
12-13 cups stuffing
½ teas pepper
1 teas thyme
2 eggs beaten
4 c. chen broth

Mix melted oleo - celery, onion
spices - eggs & broth - add
stuffing & stir - crock pot
High 45 min - reduce to
low 6 hrs - add water if
needed -

Here's what's cookin': Ck. or turkey Bake

Recipe from the kitchen of: _____ Serves: _____

1 - 7 oz box crouton
4 cups diced ck. or turkey
1 small onion diced
1 1/2 tsp. salt
1/4 tsp pepper
1 cup mayonaise or Salad Dressing
4 eggs - beaten - 3 cups milk
2 cans cr. mushroom soup
Pour half of croutons in
9 x 13 pan. mix ck. onion
salt & pepper & mayonaise
& pour in croutons. All rest

of croutons & then add milk & beaten
eggs. Prepare nite B/4. B/4 placing
in oven add 2 cans soup undiluted
Bake 2 hrs. in slow oven 325°. Grate
cheese in top while hot. Maybe
frozen B/4 soup is added on top.

61

Pork Chop Casserole
9 X 13 pan - 350° - Bake 1½ hr.

4 pork chops .   2 red apples -

2 large onions -   1 C apple cranberry
                                                    juice
Oil for cooking

5 potatoes - small   ¼ C apple jelly (melted)

Coat pk chops with flour / brown on both sides in oil - put on plate - cook rings of onions until lite brown - about 10 min, only. Meanwhile - Slice potatoes about ¼" thick. Cut apples in wedges - Arrange potatoes in bottom - Sprinkle salt & pepper - In a side dish - mix cranapple juice d 1 tbs flour - Add to fried onions * stirring any brown bits from bottom of skillet. Spoon over the potatoes. Tuck pk. chops d apple wedges into onion casserole - Cover with foil - Brush the pk chops with melted apple jelly -

Recipe for: _Easy hot dish_

from the kitchen of: _____

Rice Hot Dish

1 lb. hamb - Browned
1 c chopped celery   Salt
1 sm. onion chopped   &
2 tbls. soy sauce   pepper
1 can cken noodle soup
1 can cr. of mushroom soup   serves: ____
1 - 4 oz mushrooms -
2 cups hot water
½ cup uncooked rice
combine all - pour into greased
casserole - mix well -
Bake 300° for 1½ hrs.
Keep covered - Stir several times
while baking.

Good for meal with Ta Ta

63

Burger Logs

2 lbs Hamb — onion   salt &
1 pkge Sausage.   pepper
   Mix all together — Make into logs
& wrap each in bacon. Lay & bake
in single layer — 350° - 30-35 min —
   Turn once in you want. Length of
baking depends on size of log.

Heidi Dat Dish

   350° - 45 min — grease 9 X 13
Mix all together :
   8   oz hash Browns
         fried hamb —
I know you dont like onions — so skip !!
3/4 cup peas — Neil dont like peas so she
1 can Mushroom soup mixed (put in a few —
3/4 cup milk — Mix with soup —
6 slices cheese on top, lay on top —
   Cover with foil — Bake — (he last over)

10 minutes sprinkle with can of
      French Onions — (Sorta Break Up)
Just a little, Jimmy !!!
Rea   oud Mr. Jimbo the co   !

64

Pork Chop - dish

6 or more pk. chops Browned
Salt & pepper -
Combine - 1 can cr of celery soup
½ c - milk - ½ c. Sour cream -
Mix with thawed hash Browns -
Then grate 1 lb. cheddar cheese 1 can
Fr. Fr. Onions - take ½ of this
mixture & mix with hash Br. mixture
Put in 9 X 13. ~~tomatoes~~ over top put 6 pk. chops
Cover - 350° - 40 Mins
Then uncover & put rest of cheese & Fr.
fried onion mixture over pk. chops -
Leave in oven 5-10 min - uncovered.

Chicken Hot dish –

Here's what's cookin': 350° 1 hr.

Recipe from: _____

1 Cut Up Chicken cooked.

1½ cup celery
1 med. onion
1 C velveeta cheese
3 eggs
½ teas salt
1 C min. rice
4 C Bread crumbs.
2 cans chicken Soup
1 Can milk   Serves: 12

Chips & Butter.

Cabbage Hot dish Casserole –

Fry ~~bacon~~ Bacon – leave a little
                            unfried.

Put cabbage –
Then Bacon   2 tsp, dry
Then Cabbage again   mustard
Then Bacon   1 teas salt
Cabbage again –   1 tbls. flour
                              mix together

... top of ... cabbage + middle
sprinkle flour mixture – Then end up
with Bacon on top.

1 cup cream – put in oven for
    1 or 1½ hr. 350°.

Go on the cream maybe a
little ~~less~~ more than a cup.
could try onion if desired.

66

Creamy Chicken Hot Dish
  2 celery ribs chopped
  1 small onion
  1 tbls ole
  1 1/2 cups mayo
  1 can cr. chken soup undiluted
  1 cup frozen peas thawed
  1 tbls- lemon juice
  1 teas- salt — 2 cups cooked rice
  3 cups cubed cooked chkn   over

In small skillet - saute onion + celery
Stir in chken + rice - greased 11 X 7 pan
sprinkle with potatoe chips
  Bake 350° for 25-30 min.

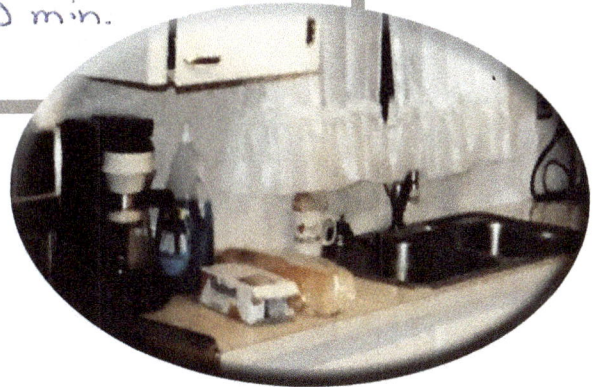

67

Chkn / Long grain Rice Bake –
1 can Mushroom Soup – 1 cup water
¾ C uncooked reg. long grain rice
¼ teas. Salt, paprika – Sprinkle pepper
4 or 5 pieces of skinless, boneless
Chkn breasts – I cut in 3"- 4" pieces
In 2 quart baking dish mix soup –
rice – water – paprika – salt & pepper (own)
Place Chkn on top – Cover –
Bake at 350° ~~~~ till done.
45 to 50 min,

Recipe From: **Cabbage/Ham Dash** Makes: _____

1/2 c. chopped onion
2 cups chopped cabbage
3/4 c. shredded carrot -
1 tbls. ole
1 2 o. (2 1/4 cups) cooked ham chopped
2 cups chopped cooked potatoes

1 teas. Worcestershire sauce
1/8 teas. pepper

In 10" skillet cook onion, cabbage & carrot
& the ole vegie are tender, stir in ham &
potatoes Worcestershire sauce & pepper. Spread
mixture evenly in skillet. Cook over medium
heat for 5 min, turning occasionally with spatula.

Cabbage Hot dish Casserole -
   1 1/2 hr or less - 350°   9 X 13 or lesser pan
Fry 1 lbr. <u>drain</u> - chopped up b/4 frying -

Put cabbage (head or whatever) chopped
Then layer cabbage - sprinkle some bacon
Then cabbage - Sprinkle between 1st & last
layer - Bacon on top = 2 tsp. dried mustard
Then on top - 1 1/4 c <u>cream</u>   1 teas. salt
Maybe a little less.   2 tbls. flour
If you desire a little onion - or cheese at the end

Broccoli Hot Dish
I make ½ of this

1 cup rice cooked only 10 min.
1-20 oz Broccoli Cuts (frozen)
1 chopped onion
1 cup grated cheese
2 cans mushroom soup
1½ sticks ole - use some of this
    to saute onions. Put Casserole -

350° - 40 min -

Broccoli Hot dish. → frozen
2 pkg broccoli - chopped - thawed. Drained -
¼ c onion

6 tbls. ole	Saute onion in the ole -
2 tbls. flour	Stir in floured water &
½ c water	cook until thickens.
1 cup cheese	Add cheese - Combine
3 eggs -	sauce & broccoli - add eggs.
	Bake at 350 - 35-40
	min - Didnt say size of
	pan.

Broccoli Casserole
10 oz frozen broccoli - cook & drain
Prepare Stove Top dressing
1 Sm. chez whiz - add to broccoli hot
Blend all & cook 45 min - 350°
    grease pan -

Swedish Meatballs.

1 lb. hamb..   ½ lb. pork.
½ c cracker crumbs   ½ tsp. pepper
½ tsp nutmeg   2 tbls - salt
2 tsp sugar   ½ tsp. ginger
1 well beaten egg - add last
    - enuf milk to moisten -

Make meat balls - roll in flour & brown
Make juice of 1 qt water - 1 pkge onion
Soup mix - Bake browned meat
balls & juice for 1 hr - 300°.
Make gravy from the juice when
ready to serve .

Crock Pot Chen.

3 pieces chen breast
1 pkge onion soup.
1 can chen Soup
1 can cr. celery Soup

Combine soups - Put
in crock the chen 1st
Then soups over chen.
Set temp on low -
Serve with rice -
          8-10 hrs

Broccoli Dot Dish.   (Rosie)
1 cup raw rice (cooked)
1-20 oz pkg Broccoli (cuts) frozen -
1- chopped onion
1 cup grated cheese.
2 cans mushroom soup -
1½ stick ole or butter
   Use some ole to saute onions
Cook rice 10 minutes only -

350° for 40 min.

Sauerkraut Dot dish -   8x8
                              9 x 13
                        salt-
Hamburger - fried - on bottom
celery-   onion + celery- ½ c onions
Sauerkraut - 1 can juice + all

Thin noodles 2 cups- broken up
     uncooked -
1 Mushroom Soup + ~~milk~~
1 celery Soup -   1 cup water

last half hr sprinkle with
  cheese I use mixture of -
      cheddar + mozarella
350- 45 min. then add cheese
                for 15 min -

Hash Brown Hot Dish - 350° - 1 hr -

Big - 9 X 13 - & mix in larg bowl.

Melt 1/3 cup ole

1 - 2 lb. bag. hash Browns

1 can potato Soup

1 can celery Soup

2 tbls. chopped onion

1 - 8 oz sour cream

1 tsp salt - = little less

1/4 pepper Teas -

mix all together
Mix 1/3 cup melted
ole + 2 or more
cups Corn flakes.
Put over the top

(over)

1 1/2 cup Shredded cheese

Carolyns - chen hot dish -
~~Betterick~~ 6 chen Breasts - fry -
Cut in pieces ~~and~~ put in greased 9X13
pan -
Take 1 pt sour cream - 2 chen cr. Soup
mix together - Pour over top of chen -
Crush 1 row of rit, crackers - put on top
Melt 2 sticks butter or ole & drizzle
over crackers -
3 teas. poppy seed - Sprinkle over top
350° - 30 - 45 min. Serve over rice o' plain

BarB Qued -
Pork Chops
- 4 in 8X8 pan - 350° - 1½hr or less -
Pour over mixture of Bar B Que
sauce - ¾ C water - Cover with
foil - turn PRchops over in the
liquid about once -
I put Baked potatoes in with
the meal - Save sauce & put back
in the bottle,

Crock Pot Dish-
    7 hrs - on low -
    4 cken Breasts
    2 pkge Stuffing Mix - 1 pkg?
1 can Cream of cken Soup
1 cup Sour cream   } together
1 cup water
Pour over 2 top items then add
Frozen green String Beans

If you want 4 hrs. on high

Spinach Ricotta Pie

375°   (you can use cot cheese)
                          instead
The Crust: Cut together 1 cup flour
(⅘ white plus ⅕ wheat is nice) &
⅓ cup ole. About 3 tbls. cold water
or enuf so that the mixture holds
together.

  Filling:
1 lb. (2 cups ricotta or cottage cheese
3 beaten eggs

½ (1 cup) chopped Spinach - 1 tbls sut.
   1 diced onion - ½ tsp: salt   Basi
S. auteed in ole/salt/pepper -
3 tbls. flour   - Dash nutmeg
½ c sharp grated cheese
Mix everything together, Blending well.
Put in unbaked pie shell, top w. 1 cup
sour cream - spread to edge of crust -
(Sour cream is optional,
Bake 375° - 40-45 min,

Mandarin cken Breasts Breasts

4 cken Breasts
1 env. dry onion Soup Mix
1-8 oz pineapple crushed undrained
1-11 oz Mandarin oranges undrained

Brown cl - combine the rest - pour over
ckl - 350-40-50 min -

Lazy No Peek Chicken -

                Greased   350°
1 cup Minute Rice   9X13
8 -10 pieces raw cken
  1 can Mushroom Soap
  1 can cr - of cken   mix
  1½ cup milk   together
  Beat & pour over cken Sprinkle
1 pkge onion Soup mix - 2 hrs

Silverware and Dishes

Blanche's Salads

Best Ever Potato Salad!!!

Potato Salad

About - ¾ c Salad dressing

¼ c cream.

1 tsp - mustard.

½ c sugar -

1½ tsp vinegar -

Sorta on this order depends on how big a batch you make -

Probably not so much go - if you - (over)

potatoes
radishes
onions
eggs
Some people put in
celery - gr - pepper - even cucs -

Stir the potato salad before serving -

Salt & pepper more if you want -

9 Day Coleslaw -

1 cup vinegar   2 teas celery seed
½ c oil   2 teas. sugar
                     ½ teas salt

Put in sauce pan - bring to boil - coo
Set aside -
Coleslaw - Shred 3 lbs or what ever -
onion - gr. pepper - 2 cups sugar - Let sta
until Sugar dissolves. Pour cooled dres
over cabbage - Keep refrigerated -

Tuna Crunch Salad (Porky)

1 can tuna
3 tbsp. dill pickle (chopped)
1 tblsp. onion - chopped (onion)
                          or chopp
½ c mayonnaise
1 tblsp. lemon juice
1½ crisp cup shredded cabbage
1 small can shoestring potatoes

Serve on lettuce

Deviled eggs & slices tomato & dill
                              pick

        Make nite B/4   Flo
Salad
2 pkg Instant vanilla pudding
add. 2 cups Buttermilk
then - 2 cans Drained - cut up
        mandarin oranges.
Then add 1 - 12 oz of cool whip
refrig. Crush 1 pkg shortbread
cookies with it - not to fine -
Fold in to other mixture &
save some for topping

Curly pasta — 16 oz or less —
1 c mayo 1 cup chopped cucumber
        1/2 cup red pepper —
        1 1/2 cup cheddar cheese
        1/2 cup chopped onion
        1/2 teas salt

Cook pasta — drain —
    Chill B/4 serving —
  Mix in large bowl & cover

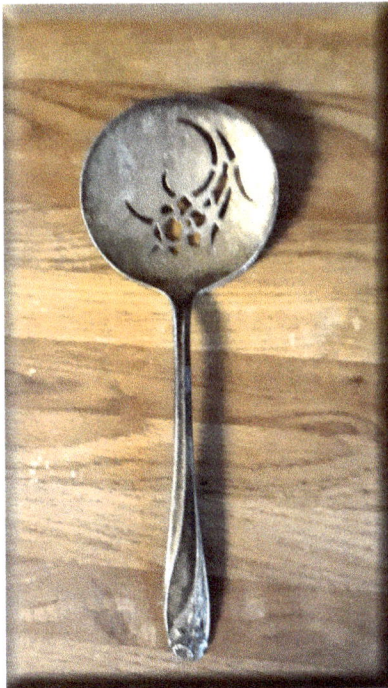

Spinach Mushroom Salad.
1 lb. fresh Spinach
1/4 lb. fresh mushrooms
1 egg white — hard boiled
1/4 cup Tarragon vinegar
2 tbls. water
1/8 teas. pepper
1/8 teas paprika
1 tbls. undiluted frozen orange juice
Trim/wash Spinach — put in bowl —
Wash/slice mushrooms add to Spinach
Combine vinegar, water, pepper —
    paprika — orange juice conc —
  Pour over Salad.

Vegie Medley.

1 - 16 oz frozen broc - carrots cauliflower
combination. I buy a head of Cauliflower &
put about 1½ cup more in recipe.

1 can mushroom soup	mix together
1 c - shredded Swiss cheese	use ⅓ of it in mixture
⅓ C sour cream	
1 jar pimento (optional)	½
1 can Fren Fried Onions	Can of this

Combine - veges + soup mixture

Put in 8 x 8 or 9 x 9 or covered Casserole. Bake
at 350° - 30 min. Top with other
half cup of the cheese & ½ can of
Fr. Fried onions. Bake uncovered
for 5 - 10 min.

Good.

Fruit Salad.
1 can mandarin oranges - cut
1 can - pineapple chunks. cut
1 can sliced peaches - cut
3 Bananas _ 2 unpeeled apples - bite size
Sauce - In
   1 pkg instant vanilla Pudding Mix
   1 cup milk
   ⅓ c frozen orange juice - Thawed
   ¾ C sour cream -
Combine all fruit - fold in Sauce mixture
Cover / chill - 3 - 4 hrs -

84

Seven Layer Salad.
1 head lettuce slice like cole slaw
1/4 C celery chopped
1/4 C gr pepper chopped
1/4 C Spanish onion chopped.
small peas - any amt.
1 cup mayo 1 tblsp. Sugar
8 strips Bacon fried - 1/2 - 3/4 small peas
Shredded cheddar cheese

Chen Pasta Salad. Poppy Seed.
1 1/2 cup twists or curly cue. Pasta -
1 1/2 cup cubed Chen.
3/4 cup Red or green grapes halves -
1/2 cup sliced celery (thin)
1/2 cup poppy seed dressing

Macroni Fruit Salad
2 eggs   1/2 cup lemon juice
1/3 cup Sugar   Boil all 4 ingred till
1 tbls flour   thick - Cool & add
                      1/4 pt - whipped cream
Filling
    drained   1 Can mandarin oranges
               1 can Crushed pineapple
               1 Box ring macroni
1/2 bag - Marshmallow - small ones

If desired cherries - yes -
    Apples & Bananas -

Pasta Salad - Vermichili -

8 oz of Vermichili noodles.
        Cook - Drain - cool. -
1 Bottle of zesty Italian dressing.
3 or 4 tbls. Shilling Salad
      Supreme Seasoning Spice.
chopped tomatoes
3-4 green stem onions.
Some green pepper - Make day ahead,
   Keep cool. -

Here's what's cookin': Carrot ~~Onions~~ Salad
Recipe from: _____

6 cups cooked carrots - cut
1 green pepper cut
1 onion chopped   } mix with
2 stalks celery chopped } cooked carrots

Marinate in 1 Can tomato soup
    3/4 cup oil   mix
    1 tablespoon prepared mustard well
    1 tbls. warcestershire   Beater
    1 cup sugar
    3/4 cup vinegar   till blended -

Cucumber Salad

8–10 cucs sliced. peeled.
I do many more.
1 cup celery. any amt.
1 ~~cup~~ green pepper. I only do half.
1½ tbls salt. Put in bowl &
mix. let stand ½ hr. drain
     liquid off. Then add.

in a bowl.
    2 cups Sugar
    1 cup vinegar
    1 teas. celery Seed
    1 teas mustard Sed.
After a day. gets to much
juice. So I drain off a lot.

Tuna Salad.   (Mom's)
    1 Box Shell noodles (small)
    2 - can tuna drained well
    1- 2. Stalks celery
    2 tbls, relish
½ cup onion - / 1 cup peas.
    1 cup miracle whip
    Start with ½ of ¼ cup sugar
    1 tsp. lemon juice
Pour half dressing & let sit over niter
    Mays need more.-

Grape Salad - (refrigerate)
Bowl Both Kinds
Mixture   green & purple grapes
            Wash - take off stems -
Make Syrup of
    ¾ cup Br. Sugar | probely
    1 cup sour cream | wont use
    ½ cup Cool whip | all this
Slivered almonds (optional) | syrup -

Rasberry Salad
Mix togther:
    1 - 8 oz Cool whip
   2 yogurt (Brand yoplate)
      Rasberry flavored
1 - Box dry white chocolate Pudding mix
      Sugar free — or regular
Justt B/4 Serving add -
   1 or more fresh ~~Box~~ resberies -
   or Dole frozen rasberries -
Jill added a hand full blue berries - "over
Try:
Peach yogurt - + fresh or canned
            peaches -
_____

Strawberry yogurt + Strawberrys

Salads

Rainbow Pasta Salad
8 oz Curlie - cooked - drained & cooled
                                    Macroni
2 cans - Shrimp - drained -
½ cup nuts - (optional)
¼ c French Salad dressing
¼ c mayo
2 tbsp. stuffed pimento green olives
1 teas. chopped onions - Combine & cover -
refrig at least 2 hrs.

Broccoli/Cauliflower - Raisen Salad
½ c sugar   } mix dressing
¼ c vinegar   } together.
1 c Hellmans' Mayonaise
½ lb. chopped Browned Bacon
6 or less bite sized pieces brocoli (1 cup)
1 head cauliflower - Bite sized pieces
½ cup chopped onion.
½ cup or less raisins
½ cup pecans or less   (over)

Pour Dressing over nite b/4. If
serving at supper - I put on in A.M.
Keep covered & refrigerated.

90

Shrimp Salad.

1 pkge ring macroni - cooked / drained
        Put in frig to cool -
2 pkge frozen deveined shrimp -
   or 1 can & 1 frozen -
1 can Le Seur peas -
1½ c diced celery
2 tbls - gr. pepper ⎫ diced -
2 tbls onion   ⎭
Mayo - sweet pickle juice & a
little cream

or cuc -
    Tomato -

Butter Milk Cookie Salad -
1 cup buttermilk
1 - (3¾oz) Instant vanilla pudding
+½ cups cool whip -
1 Carton Coolwhip
1 can mandarin oranges
1 small crushed pineapple ??
¼ pkg - more choc stripe cookies
      broken into small pieces -
Blend buttermilk - pudding - Add

Work Out Spinach / Cottage Cheese

10 oz. (1/2) pkg chopped Spinach / I think
1 Scallion sliced thin   did double
1/3 teas. gr. nutmeg   this recipe.
    Water –
1/2 c. low fat cottage cheese
1/4 Teas oregano. 1/8 teas. rosemary.
Cook Spinach, scallion & nutmeg in small
amt of water – 5 min –
Drain – spread over bottom of baking dish
top with cheese & spices   over –
    Bake 350° – 15 min.

Oh! yeah! yeah! yeah!
    114 calories
    16.7. protein
    6.6 grams carbohydrate
    2 grams fat –

Judy's Summer Salad -

1 Box ring macronie - cooked
drained & cooled in cold water -

Cut up - ½ c carrots -
    ½ c. green onion top + onion
    ½ cup gr. pepper
½ cup unpeeled chopped cucumber
½ cups chopped celery -
Mix all these together & Put on

dressing of
3/4 cup Salad dressing
3/4 cup sugar
2 tbspoons vinegar
1/8 teas. ginger

Blanche with her family. Back row: Blanche, Madelyn, Nick, Florence, Bernice,
Front row: Tootie, Stepmother Hazel, "Daddy," and Cunda

cKen Salad (Vorky)

1½ c - Rosamarina   6 c diced cKen
4 c. celery.   1 c. slivered
1 diced onion   almonds
½ diced green pepper
1 tbls. real lemon
2 tsp salt
½ tsp pepper -
½ tsp. mustard
½ tsp paprika - pimente
2 cans Mandarin oranges   (over)
Dressing - 2 c. mayonaise
          ½ c whipping cream -

Cook Rosamorina in salt water as
directed. Rinsed chill. combine celery,
onion - gr. pepper - lemon juice -
salt/pepper. mustard. paprika in bowl.
Fold in oranges/cKen - Mix with
dressing - B/4 serving add 1 cup almonds

Macroni Salad from loots.

Cherry tomatoes + Long spagetti -
1 cucumber cubed. Cook - Drain -
½ bunch winter onions. sliced -
½ bunch celery - chopped -
1 Bottle Italian dressing -
1 Salad Supreme spices Seasoning.
Stand 3 -5- hrs. Cool.

Broccoli / Cauliflower - Raisen Salad
½ c sugar   mix dressing
¼ c vinegar   together.
1 c Hellmans' Mayonaise
½ lb. chopped Browned Bacon
6 or less bite sized pieces brocoli (1 cup,
1 head cauliflower - Bite sized pieces
½ cup chopped onion.
½ cup or less raisins
½ cup pecans or less   (over)

Pour dressing over nite b/4. If
serving at supper - I put on in A.M.
Keep covered & refrigerated.

Here's what's cookin': **Italian Veg Salad**

Recipe from: _____

Large bowl w/ tite ftg. cover

1 Med. cuc. sliced
8-10 sliced radishes
1-2 carrots sliced
3/4 to 1/2 gr. pepper chopped coarse
1/4 - 1/2 cup onion
1/2 - 3/4 cauliflower Broken
    into flowerettes
1/2 - 3/4 can Blk & green olives
1/2 cup chopped celery
2 lge raw mushrooms

Use some Italian
dressing to marinate
(At least 6 hrs)

Sprinkly 1/4 cup
Parmesan cheese
over it just B/4
serving

Serves: _____

🌱 96

Cookie Salad

1 pkge stripped cookies –

3/4ths in pieces Set aside
2 pkge Instant vanilla pudding
2 cups Buttermilk –
2 – 11 oz mandarin oranges.
16 oz cool whip
Beat pudding & Buttermilk Together
Fold in Cool whip – Add oranges &

1 can crushed pineapple if desired –
Add cookies crushed
Keep Salad in frig

The Family

Blanche's Soups

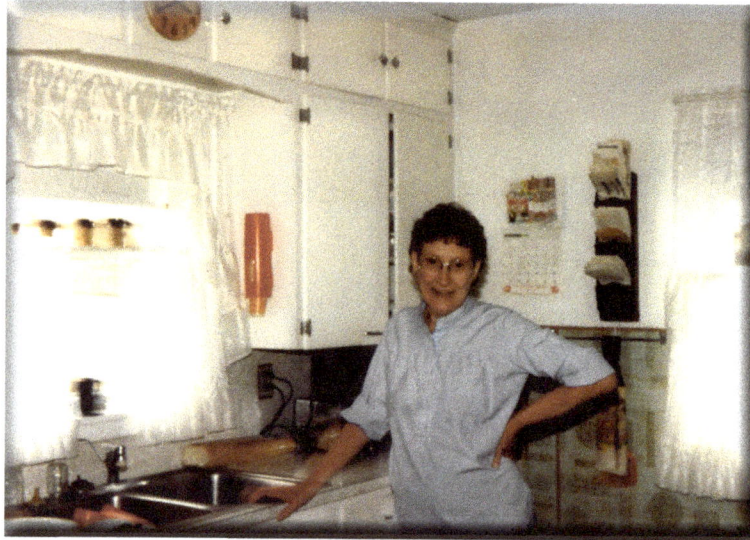

Quik Veggie Soup
1 lbs. hamburger (Browned)   1 Teas-
1 onion diced   thyme
4 - potatoes chopped-   6 cups water-
4 - carrots chopped   1 jar qt. tomato
1 cup pearled Barley - uncooked   whole -
6 Beef bouillion cubes.
    Add all ingredients - Bring to Boil
Reduce heat till veggiables tender -
    about 45 min.

    Boil all carrots & all ingred.
for 1½ hrs - or more -

Roast Beef Barley Soup

1 cup celery – carrots & onion (½ cup
1 tbls ole –
4 cups beef broth
4 cup water
2 cups chopped cooked beef
1 can diced tomatoes
1 cup quick cooking barley
½ teas, oregano – dried basil
½ cup peas.

Cheese & Potato Soup

½ c. wild rice - uncooked
1½ cups water
½ lb. bacon - fry - cut in pieces drain
¼ c. - chopped onion
2 - 10¾ oz cans cream of potato soup
  (dilute with 1 can liquid (½ milk ½ water)
1 qt. milk
2 ½ cups grated Am. cheese -
  combine rice/water in saucepan &
cook over low heat for 45 min.

Drain - Set Aside. fry Bacon/onion until
crisp - Drain - Put soup in lg ~~sauce~~ pan.
dilute as directed - Stir in qt milk. Bacon
nion - cheese & cooked rice Stir in
cheese until melted

Potato Soup
3 cups peeled & cubed potatoes
2 cups milk
2 cups frozen Calif blend vegies
1 lb. Amer. cheese spread - cubed
3 tbls. ole. Salt & Pepper
Put potatoes in kettle with 4 cups water
bring to boil - reduce heat - cover - simmer
10 to 15 min - drain - add milk & vegies.
Bring to ~~boil over gentle heat~~ gentle boil
over med heat - reduce heat - add
cheese, ole & seasoning. Heat over low
heat - stirring frequently until cheese
is melted & vegies are tender crisp.
Serve with grated Parmesan cheese -
Make 6 - one cup servings.
If desired dice 2 cans (15 oz) whole
potatoes into cubes.

CKen Noodle Soup

1 cKen - 2½ qts water
1 cup diced carrots
1 cup diced celery
2 ~~salt~~ Reas cKen granules
   ¼ cup chopped onions
   ¼ teas marjoram + salt
   ¼ teas thyme + pepper
   1 Bay Leaf
   1½ cup uncooked thin noodles

Large saucepan place 11 first Ingredients
Bring to Boil - skim off foam & Reduce
heat. cover - simmer for (-)½ hrs -
Remove from broth - cKen - allow to cool -
DeBone cKen. dice - add noodles - cook extil
tender - Remove Bay leaf 3/4 serving - add
cKen pieces

his elbow. So goes in to the Dr. for his elbow. last words when he left with Nancy! Judy. See Thurs. Mom for pancakes & cribbage. me know how you make out with Cathie her address I'll send Connie a card.
it goes on! Thanks Again for all the
now know it will never happen again.

Love ya all
Mom.

with them. I'm
till you Flo came. Ginger informed me
years of paying her room over W.W.N. She is
Welfare. And she was rich. So she
gang sure gets together a lot! lot! Even
strange soup. So all were out to Deide's
sometimes wondering if they have any
was out & went for his classmate
R. Mahoney!!

Rind of beef
3 Ribs and
about 4 or 5
Brings them
Baby sitting
to see them
Well think

Bean & Ham Soup

8 cups water - also 1 32g Chen broth - Basil 1 Teas
1 chopped cup onion - 1 cup celery ½ tbls salt
2 cups carrots - 2 cups potatoe - Cook
till done. about 1½ - 1 hr.
1 - 1 jar lg whole tomatoes & 28oz. pk.
Beans

Veg Soup - Porky -

1# ground meat
4 c chop cabbage - (½ small head)
2 large onions
2 stalks celery
6 carrots
2 med potatoes
2 Tbls - dried parsley flakes
1 - 6 oz tomato paste
2 - 9 lb. can tomato

2 can beef broth
4 soup cans water
1 tbls - salt
½ tsp pepper
1 tbls - sugar
Br - meats - add other ingre
Simmer 2 hrs or longer -

107

Blanche's Desserts

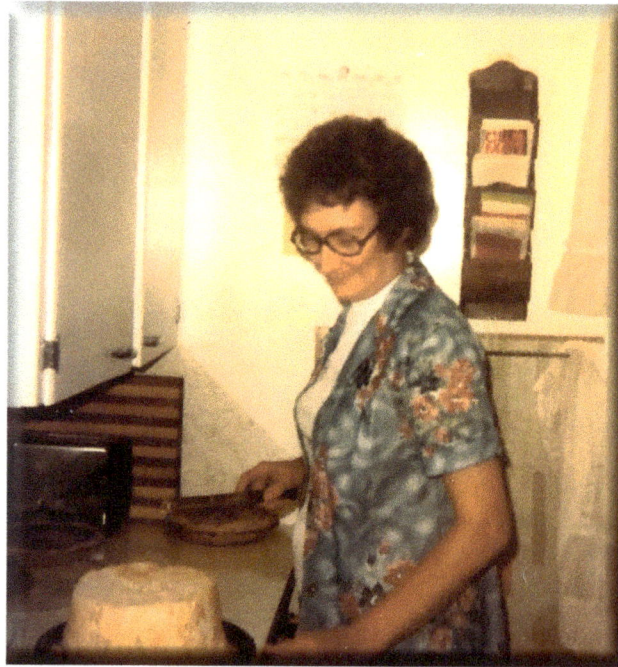

Rhubarb Dessert - grease

1st layer -
1/2 cup milk
2 teas Baking Powder
1 1/2 cup flour
1/4 tsp. salt
1 egg
2 tbls -oil

2nd - Rhubarb 3 cups

3rd
1 1/4 cup milk
3 eggs
1 1/2 teas vanilla
1 1/4 cup sugar
Pour on top
Dot some of
1st layer on top

Bake - 1 hr.

Banna Bread - Su Sis
3/4 cup white Sugar -
1/2 c shortening
2 eggs   350°
2 c flour   50-60 min -
1 tsp. Soda
1/2 tsp. salt -
1 cup mashed bannae -

Zuchini Bread - 325° - 1 hr
3 eggs - 1 cup oil   grease pans
2 cups Sugar -   (7 - 3 15 pans)
2 teas cinnomon
1 - Teas - Baking soda - salt
1/4 teas - Baking powder
3 Teas - vanilla - 2 cups zuchini
3 cups flower

Grate zuchini with skin

Recipe: Pumpkin Loaf - 6 small or 3 lge -
From: _____ Makes: _____
1 cup Mazola oil - 3 c Sugar
Can Pumplin -   3 1/3 c flour
                      1/2 tsp Baking powder
4 eggs - 2 Tsp. Baking Soda
                      2 teas cinnamon
1 Teas each cloves & nutmeg
1 1/2 teas. salt - 350°. 1 hr.

©CURRENT, INC.

110

Cherry Rhubarb Crunch -

1 c oatmeal - 1 c Br. Sugar ½ teas. salt
1 c flour - cut in ½ cup ole. Pat 2 cups
of this in greased 9 X 13 pan. Cover with
4 cups rhubarb. Sauce pan 1 cup sugar
2 tbls - cornstarch. 1 cup water Cook until
thick & clear - Stir in 1 Teas almond extract.
& 1 can cherry pie filling. Spoon over
rhubarb - Combine ½ c nuts into the reserved
crumb mixture. Sprinkle over cherries -
Bake 350° - 40-45 min.

Rhubarb Crunch 9X9
Mix until crumbly -
1 c flour - oatmeal, br. sugar -
   1 teas cinnamon ½ c melted ole.

Press ½ in pan - greased. Cover with
4 cups diced rhubarb -
   Combine 1 c sugar - 1 c water } cook
1 teas vanilla 2 tbls cornstarch }
Pour over rhubarb - top with remaining
crumbs - 350° - 35° - 40 - Coolwhip or
                              ice cream

½ Recipe Rhubarb Custard -

½ c Sugar	mix all	add together
½ c milk	these	2 eggs -
2 tsp Bak Powder	to -	1¼ c Sugar
1½ c flour	gether	1¼ c milk
pinch salt	& spread	1½ teas vanilla
1 egg -	in pie	Beat -
2 tbls oil	pan.	Put rhubarb - 3 or 4 c.
Save ½ to put on		on top of batter &
Top of rhubarb. ½ c		then pour custard

Rhubarb Upside down -
Greased 9 X 13 - 350 - 60 - 70 min
1st - 5 cups rhubarb - chopped
2nd - 3 oz. strawberry jello
3rd - 1 cup sugar
4th - 3 cups mini marshmallows
5a - yellow cake mix (make as on pkg.)
drizzle over 4 mixtures of ingred -
when done - let set about 10-15 min -
flip on 12 X 15 pan - serve cool whip
eas.

Recipe for: Layered Rhubarb
from the kitchen of: Cake
6-5 cups rhubarb cut up
Then sprinkle strawberry or
        cherry 3 g - jello over
rhubarb -
   Then 1 c. Sugar
3 cups miniature Marshmellow
1 - D. H. or Betty Crocker white
cake mix - Make as   serves:
cake & pour over marsmellow
Bake in greased 9 X 13 pan
about 50 minutes - 350°
Let pan set for about 20 min
Then tip over on 12 X 15 pan
& piece of wax paper -
Serve with cool whip -

Strawberry Dessert - 9 X 13

From the kitchen of...

2 pkg strawberry jello
2½ c boiling water
Add 2 pkge frozen strawberries small
Stir until starting to stiffen
Spoon over ½ broken up angel food
Cake. Last 3rd of jello. Add 1
cup Cool whip & cover over other
⅓ on Top.

Here's what's cookin'; **Rasberry Dessert**

Recipe from:

2½ cups crushed pretzels
¾ c. melted butter
3 tbls. Sugar
Combine & put in 9 X 13 pan
Bake at 375° - 10 min. cool

1 - 8 oz Phil cream cheese
1 cup sugar   mix with
1 tsp. vanilla   fork

Whip 1 pkg dream whip
½ cup milk

---

add to cream cheese +
spread on crust.

Dissolve 2 pkge (3oz)
rasberry jello
2 cups hot water
add 2 Boxes frozen
raspberries

Set until jelly
+ put over cream
mix - refrigerate

whip cream if desired

Serves:

Coco Hole drop cake.

1 white cake mix - 9 X 13 greased pan
Make as cake - Cool
Poke holes with wooden spoon -
Pour Coco casta in holes & drizzle
rest over the cake -
Then cover with 12 oz Cool whips
+ coconut sprinkled over top 3/4 cup
Keep refrigerated.

Choc Cake -   9 X 13 greased
                                           350°
  1 - choc cake mix
  4 eggs -
  1 can (Beat it) cherry pie mix

Also -
  1 Spice cake
  4 eggs -
  1 can raisin Sour cream
           pie -

Oreo Dessert - Ken Herbek -

1 1/2 lb. crushed oreo cookies
1/2 gal softened vanilla ice cream
1 - 16 oz choc fudge sauce
  whip cream -
Grease 9 X 13 pan - Spred
oreo cookies - Then ice cream -
Beat choc very slightly to
spread over ice cream. Cover
& freeze - ~~loooooooooooooop~~
top with Cool whip 3/4 Serving.

114

Angel Sugar Crisps

1 c ole - ½ c sugar ½ c Br. Sugar
1 egg - 1 teas. vanilla - 2 c flour
1 teas. Baking Soda - cream of tartar
½ teas salt - Water.
Mix 5 - 1st ingred. Add flour soda & rest.
Shape into marble size balls. Dip ½
in water - then in Sugar. Place sugar
side up on ungreased cookie sheet.
400° - 6 min - or until done.

Pineapple Cherry Cake

1 - 20 oz crushed pineapple undrained
1 - 21 oz cherry or blueberry pie filling
1 pkge yellow cake mix
½ cup ole - Greased pan
In 9X13 pan spread pineapple over
bottom. Carefully spread pie mix.
Sprinkle dry cake mix - Dot with ole
Bake 350° - 50 or 60 mins.
Serve with Cool whip

Lemon Soda Cracker Dessert

40 Squares soda crackers crushed
        Mix with melted ole -
Pat in 9 X 13 Pan.
4 egg whites Beat Pretty stiff
        Add 1 cup Sugar
Spread over crackers - Bake 350 - ½ hr.
Let cool spread 8 oz cool whip (½ of it)
then spread canned lemon pie mix over +
Rest of cool whip - coconut if desired -

Recipe for:

Date Bars

1½ cup flour   1 cup Br. Sugar

1½ cups oatmeal   ½ tsp soda

¾ cup ole

Mix - put in 9 X 13 pan grease

3500   25 min -

Cook until thick & cool.

Pat Pat ½ of crust mixture in

bottom of pans - filling made of

1 cup dates - 1 cup water ½ c sugar 1 tablespoon flour

Spread cooled filling on top of crust
Sprinkle remainder of crust over the
top - Bake until Brown - About 25
min

`New Recipe -
9X13 Pan - greased -

1 - One Step Angel Food
1 - Can lemon pie mix
1 cup coconut (optional)
  Mix all together - Bake 350°
for 20 - 25 min - Sprinkle
with powd Sugar - when cool -

Recipe for: Mary's Berry Delight
from the kitchen of: _____
1½ c. crushed graham crackers
¼ c sugar - ⅓ c. ole
Mix these 3 Together - Press in 9X13
Put in frig to cool - Then mix
1 - 8 oz Phila cr. cheese - ¼ c sugar
2 tbls. milk. Beat together - well -
Then fold in about 6 oz. of a 12 oz
cool whip - Pour over graham crackers
& put back in frig - Then cut up
about 4 cups strawberries - put over cr.
cheese mixture - Then - 2 pkge of instant
vanilla pudding - mix with 3½ cups
milk - fold in rest of cool whip. Pour
over strawberries. I put a little
less of cool whip in each mixture.
Then when serve - put ½ of a straw -
berry on top of each piece you
serve - Keep refrigerated. Keeps for a
week or so -

Rhubarb Cake.   Delicious!!

Cream together   9 X 13 greased &
1½ cup Br. Sugar   floured pan
1 egg beaten   350° - 40 min.
½ cup Sour milk (mix 1½ tbls. vinegar in)
                (Bottom of ½ c + then fill with)
                                        milk)
1 tsp. Soda
2 cups flour
2 cups rhubarb. I put ¼ more. chop chop -
Mix all these together then B/4 baking

½ cup Sugar
1 tsp cinnamon   ½ C chopped pecans
                      or nuts -
Sprinkle all over the 9 X 13 -

    Delicious - Got it from Vicki's
new book she gave me for
Ma Da.

Strawberry, Rhubarb Coffee Cake

Filling 4½ c rhubarb - chopped
          24 oz - fzn - strawberries)
          3 tbls. lemon juice 1½ c sugar
          ½ c cornstarch -

Cake 3 c flour - 1c sugar
1 teas. salt, baking powd, vanilla
1c ole - 1c buttermilk - 2 eggs -
Topping ¾ c Sugar - ½ c flour ¼ c ole

Combine fruits & cook - covered - 5 min,
Stirring occasionally - Add lemon juice
sugar & cornstarch. Cook stirring till
thick. Cool - Make cake - Spread ½ of
batter in greased 13 X 9 pan - Spread
fruit over batter - Then add rest of batter
spread in mounds on top of filling -
Mix topping until crumbly - Sprinkle
over all - Bake 375° - 45 min.
Serve slightly warm -

Busy Day Pumpkin Dessert — grease 60-75 min. — 9X13 - 350° — pan.

1 - 30 oz pumpkin pie mix ⎫
3 eggs   ⎬ Combine these 4 together
1 c sugar   ⎪
1 (12 oz) evaporated milk ⎭

Pour into pan. Sprinkle 1 yellow cake mix over pumpkin mixture. Drizzle 1 cup melted ole or butter. Sprinkle one cup chopped pecans over ole. Bake 60-75 min or until wooden toothpick inserted in center comes out clean.

Serve with whipped cream or vanilla yogurt or ice cream.

Have your girl friends in.

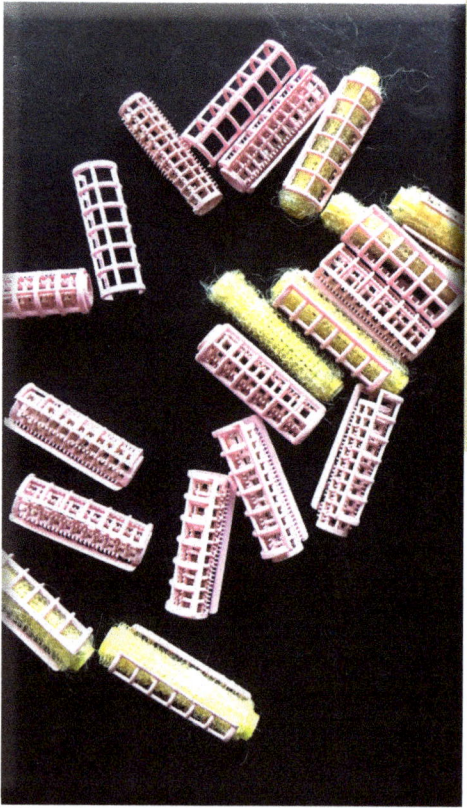

Every night Blanche rolled up her hair with plastic rollers.

Pumpkin ~~Cake~~ Pudding Cake.

9 X 13 pan - 350° 1 hr - grease pan -

1 pkg Spice Cake mix	1 tsp cinnamon
1 cup Sugar	½ tsp. ginger
¾ c. walnuts chopped	½ tsp salt
14 oz evaporated milk	¼ tsp cloves.
1 lb 3 oz size can pumpkin-	Mix altogether
3 eggs - Beaten -	Pour into 9 x 13
except nuts	pan -
	(over)

Sprinkle cake mix over top -
Sprinkle nuts (the ¾ cup) I used less.
Melt 1 stick of ole & drizzle over
top. Bake -

You can use white or yellow
or Spice cake mix
Doesn't call for whip cream or
ice cream -

Apple Centum Pie Dessert

Crust - 1¼ c crushed graham crackers
    ¼ c walnuts chopped fine   (double 9x13)
2 tbls. Br. Sugar - ¼ c ole - melted -
Crust on bottom of pan - 350° - 5 min.
Filling -
3 apples - sliced thin - 3 tbls. ole - Sautee
Stir till done -
Make filling 4 - 8 oz cream cheese 5 eggs -
½ c sour cream - ½ teas. cinnamon & nutmeg
    1 c sugar -   1 cup
Mix all these together - Then add
Sauteed Apples to it & pour over
graham cracker mixture. 350° - 1 hr.
Buy Ice cream caramel - MicroWave
& pour over each piece of cake on plates.

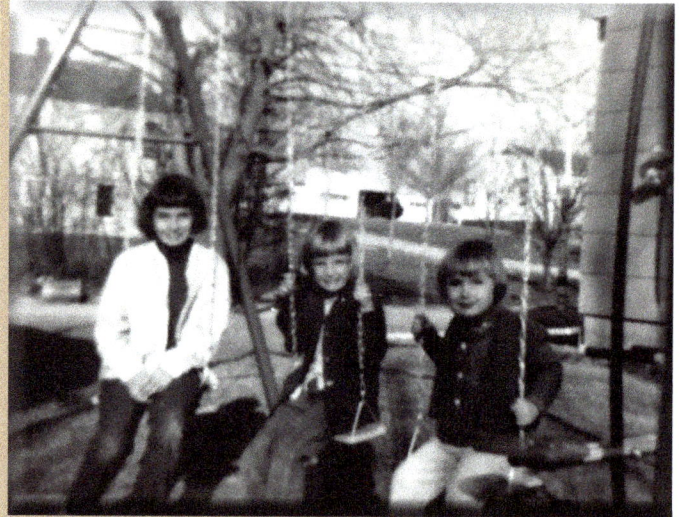

~ *Do we ever tell our kids how she made some of the best apple pie, rhubarb custard, homemade breads, buns and caramel rolls in the neighborhood?*

Recipe: Carol's Pumpkin Dessert
From: Makes:
60 to 70 min - 350° -
    9x13 greased pan -

1 - 30 oz pumpkin Mix
3 eggs   1 - 12 g Evaporated Milk
1 cup Sugar
    Mix These 4 - Put in Pan - Then

©CURRENT, INC.

sprinkle 1 yellow cake mix over
top of it. Then drizzle 1 cup melted
ole - Sprinkle 1 cup pecans (chopped)
optional -
Serve with cool whip or ice
cream - Delicious -
yogurt too.

Marshmallow Delights

NeRRi:

1 tube (8oz) refrigerated Cresent rolls.
¼ c sugar.
1 tbls. cinnomon
8 lge. marshmallows
¼ c melted ole
Seperate roll into 8 Triangles. Combine
Sugar & cinnon • Dip Marshmallows
in the melted ole. & roll in the
Sugar/cinnmon. & place on the.
Triangle. Pinch dough around the
marshmallow – seal all edges
Dip top of dough in remaining
ole & then cinnomon/sugar.
Place with sugar side up in
greased pan or muffin tins .
   350° – 375° for 13–15 min .
      Eat! Eat! Eat! Warm.

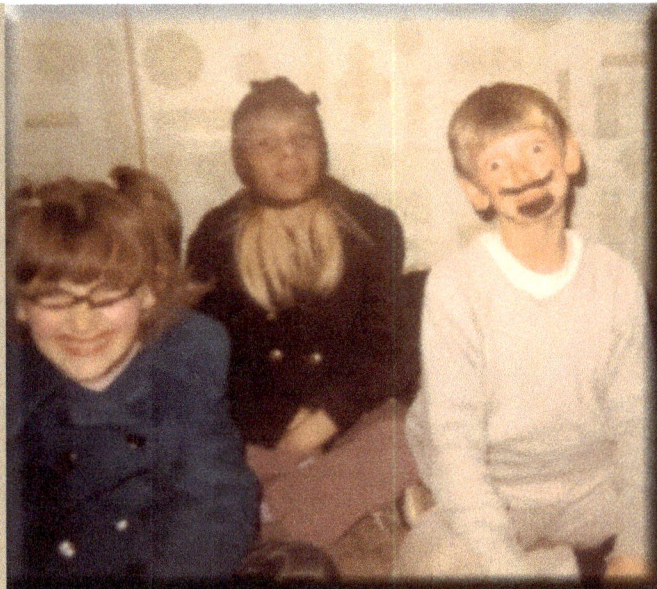

Rhubarb or. Delight Dessert.

Crust – 1 c flour. ¼ c Sugar – ⅓ c ole –
10" pie plate or 9 X 9 .
Rhubarb layer – 3–4 cups rhubarb ½ c Sugar
         combine these – 1 tbls. flour
Cream Layer – 12 oz cream cheese – 2 eggs
                  ½ c Sugar
Topping – 1 c sour cream – 2 tbls Sugar
            1 teas. vanilla
Pat in crust – Put rhubarb layer on
Crust . Bake 375° – 15 min – Meanwhile
prepare cream layer by beating together
until fluffy – Beat in eggs one at a time
Pour over hot rhubarb – Bake 350° for
30 min • Spread Toping over hot layers,
Chill –

Rhubarb Squares -

1 1/2 c flour - 3 tbls. sugar 3/4 c ole -
Mix till crumbly - Press in bottom of 9X13
Bake 350° - 10 minutes.
Filling. 3 tbls. flour. 3/4 c cream - 2 c sugar
divided - 4 eggs separated - 2 teas vanilla
5 c cut rhubarb - Blend flour + cream until
smooth - add 1 1/4 c sugar + egg yolks -
mix well. Fold in vanilla + rhubarb.
Pour into crust - Bake 325° - 60 min.
or until done. Beat remaining sugar + egg
whites until stiff - Add remaining sugar
+ beat till peaks form. top on cake + broil.

Pretzel Dessert.   Flo

3 Tbls. Sugar   - 2 cups crushed pretzels
     3/4 c melted ole -
Mix together + pat in 9 X 13 pan - at
350° for 15 min. Cool - Mix 1/2 c powd
sugar + 1 - 8 oz cream cheese - Fold in
large Cool whip - 2 c small marsh -
mallows - Spread on baked layer.
1 - 6 oz Strawberry jello + 2 1/2 c boiling
water - (I used 2 Strawberry junkets

instead - Cooked it + after thick
I added 2 or 3 cups of my fresh
sliced Strawberries - Put over top.
Keep refrigerated.
Junket worked fine instead of water
+ jello.

Dessert.   Nick/Gertie

1st layer - 1c flour - ½ c chopped nuts
        1 stick ole - mix - spread in
    9 X 13 pan - no grease - 350° - 20 min
2nd layer. 1 - 8 oz phie cr cheese -
        1 cup cool whip - 1c powd sugar
1 tsp vanilla. Put in bowl - beat.
Pour on top of baked crust.
3rd layer   2 - 3½ oz pkge of Instant
            pistachio Pudding - Put
in bowl & add 2¾c milk. beat
until thick. Pour over cream cheese
mixture. Frigerate & cool - Serve.
Use Instant puddings.
    strawberry & add top fresh ½ strawberries.
Lemon -
Coconut. Sprinkle with cocoa
Any flavor you like -

Lemon Soda Cracker Dessert -
40 sq. soda crackers - crushed
        1 stick of ole Pat in 9 X 13
4 egg whites
1 (8 oz Cool whip)
1 can lemon pie filling
1 cup Sugar in egg whites
coconut - over top - I added my burned   coco nut -
            Sprinkle coconut -

9 X 13 pan - Melt ole add to crushed
crackers - pat in pan
Beat egg whites pretty stiff - add sugar -
Spread over crackers - Bake 358° - 30 min -
let cool. (Cool whip over top ½) Then
spread lemon pie over top then rest of
Cool whip, coconut if desired - Keep in
frig.

125 🌱

Pecan Puffs   350° - 20 min

1 c ole
½ c powd sugar } mix well
1 teas. vanilla   together

add
 2 ¼ C flour   Chill & roll into
 ¼ teas. salt   balls.
3/4 C. nuts or pecans Bake 400° - 10-12 min
                      Roll in powd.
                      Sugar while warm &
                      then again when cool

Pecan Puffs [Do not refrig]
300° - 30 minutes
  1 cup butter
  4 tbls. powder sugar } mix
  1 teas. vanilla   to
                         gether

Add - 2 cups flour
      1 ½ cup pecans - chopped.

Put on cookie sheet - roll about
size walnut - Get about 40-45 (buzy)

Florence Pecan Puffs -

1 cup Butter
        powd. sugar   } mix
4 tbls white sugar   } together
1 teas. vanilla

Add 2 cups flour
     2 cups pecans -
Bake 300° - 30 min   over

Do not
refrig
dough

Must have been her favorite!

Recipe: *Favorite Dessert*

From: _____ **Makes:** _____

1 cup flour - 2 tbls. Sugar ½ c ole.
Combine & put in 9X13 - ungreased pan
Bake 10-15 min - let cool cool
Combine

8 oz cr. philia cheese) Combine & put on top
1 cup cool whip   } of crust - & spoon
1 cup Sugar   } it all over & then push
                    to corners -
                                    over →

©CURRENT, INC.

Favorite Dessert   9 X 13 Pan
                     or 1 9X9 + 1 loaf pan -

1 cup flour   ) Combine & press
2 tbls. Sugar   } in pan - Bake 350°
½ c ole   ) 15 - 10 min - COOl
Combine

8 oz cream cheese) Combine & put on
1 cup cool whip   } Cooled crust
1 cup powd Sugar)
Combine 2 Instant Lemon pudding mix
& 3 cups milk - I use skim - Pour on

Favorite Dessert

1 cup flour   ) Combine & put in bottom
2 tbls. Sugar   } 9X13 pan. Bake 350° -
½ c ole   ) 10-15 min. Cool -
Combine

8 oz cr. cheese) Combine & put on top
1 cup cool whip } of cooled - crust -
1 c powder Sugar)
Combine (2) Instant Lemon Pudding Mix
3 cups milk. Pour on top of cheese layer

top this with cool whip &
sprinkle with chopped nuts.

Could use any type of Instant
pudding -

Recipe: Rhubarb Bread —
From: Makes:

¼ c melted ole.

add ½ c orange juice   1½ cups rhubarb

½ c milk   diced small —

2 eggs   2¾ cup

1 cup sugar   flour   350° — about 50 min

1 Tbls. baking powd.

½ teas. soda, salt, nutmeg —

Rhubarb Cake or Bars —

9 X 13 greased — 350° 50 min

1½ cup sugar   2 cups flour

½ cup ole   2 cups diced rhubarb —

1 egg   ½ cup nuts (optional)

1 cup sour milk — ⅓ vinegar ¾ milk

1 teas soda + vanilla

½ teas cinnamon ½ teas. salt

Over top — 1½ teas cinnamon

½ cup or less sugar —

Sprinkle over top —

Brownies   —   (Best)

1 stick ole + 1 cup sugar

cream well —

Add 4 eggs Beat — add 1 cup flour

+ 1 lge can Hershey choc —

Bake - 30 min - 350° cool —

Frosting —

½ cup sugar ½ cup br. sugar

¼ ole cup ¼ cup milk —

Bring to boil — take off heat add 6 oz chips
cream frosting

🌱 128

Angel Food / Lemon Pie Bar

1 - Angel food cake mix - Don't
add the water. Add a
22 oz. can Lemon Pie Mix -
1 - cup coconut & optional -
Grease a jelly roll pan -
(My mistake I put in 9 X 13 -
350° - 20 - 25 min - Mite of

Poppy Seed Bread Lemon

1 lemon cake mix
1 pkg Instant Pudding ~~Vanilla~~ lemon
4 eggs
1 cup water
1/3 c. oil
1/4 cup heaping poppy seed.

350° - 45 - 50 min

Carrot Bars – 350° – 25 – 30 min –
9 X 13 Greased pan

1 cup sugar –   I mix these
3/4 cup oil   8 7 top
2 eggs –   things
1 – lge baby food carrots   well –
1 teas – vanilla   then
1 teas soda   flour –
1 teas – cinnomon
1 cup flour –   1/2 cup nuts if
                  (over)   wanted –

After baking – let cool –
Frosting = I make = phili cr.
                                cheese
                      cups
About 2 or more of
       powder sugar – 1 Teas vanilla
a dab of ole or butter –

Cream Puff Dessert -
1 C water - ½ C ole
1 C flour - 4 eggs
2 small boxes Instant pudding,
    any flavor
4 C milk
8 oz cr cheese softened
12 g whip topping
choc. souce - nuts if desired . over-

Recipe: Mix water + ole - Bring to boil, add flour
From: all at once & stir rapidly Makes til a ball
Remove from heat - cool slightly. Add eggs
one at a time - beat well after each egg.
Spread on greased 11 X 14 pan - Bake 400° for
30 min, Cool. Will look like moon surface
Dont prick- leave as is. Mix pudding
with milk. Beat in cr. cheese - Blend
till spreadable. Spread on crust, refrig
20 min. top with coolwhip. Drizzle with
    choc. souce . refrig!

131

Pistacheo Dessert

1st Layer -
1 cup flour - 1/2 c walnuts -
1 stick ole - mix & spread 9 X 13 pan

350° - 15 min. cool crust

2nd Layer -
1 8oz pkge of cr. cheese - 1 cup cool whip
1 cup powd sugar - 1 tsp vanilla
put in bowl & beat - pour on crust.

3/rd layer

2 - 3 1/2 oz pkg - Pistacheo Instant pudding.
Put in bowl & add # 2 3/4 cups milk
beat until thick - pour over cr. cheese
mixture. cool & serve with whip
cream if ~~they~~ you want.

Mini Elephant Ears -
Be Careful -

Frozen white dinner roll dough -
  Heat oil in deep Kettle - 2"or 3" -

Thaw dough for 2 hrs. Heat oil.
Combine 1/2 cup ~~Sugar~~ - 1 tbls. cinnamon
Set aside - Stretch each piece of dough
into flat ears - Fry a couple
at a time - 1 1/2 min. per side or until
Brown Drain on paper towel. Brush
with 3 or 4 tbls. melted ole -
Sprinkle Sugar & cinnamon mixture.
delicious -

Almond Bars -
Crust - 1 cup ole   Combine & put
        2 c flour   in 9 x 13 -
        1/2 c powd. Sugar Bake 350
                           20-25 min -

Filling -
8 oz cream cheese   Beat together - Pour
2 eggs   over crust while hot.
1/2 c white Sugar   15-20 min -
1 teas. Almond extract   350° - cool.
                           & cut
              (over)

Frosting
1 1/2 cup powdered sugar
1/4 c ole
1 teas. Almond extract
1 1/2 tblsp. milk

~ Do we ever tell our kids what a strong woman Grandma Blanche must have been to be going through grief over the death of her husband while having some of her children acting in rebellious ways, and how she she prayed every night that they would come home safely?

~ Do we ever tell our kids how she left the bathroom light on with a list of names so that we could cross off our name when we came in and the last one would shut off the bathroom light, and then she could sleep peacefully?

Dream Bars

1 tbls - ole - ½ c milk
2 eggs - 1 c Sugar - 1 c. flour
1 tsp. vanilla ½ teas . salt
1 tsp. Baking powder.
Beat milk + ole together until milk is hot but not boiling. Beat eggs d Sugar until lite - Stir in vanilla
Mix flour - salt & Baking powder together. Add flour mixture to egg mixture. Alternating with Milk/ ole. Gently fold until smooth.
greased 9 X 13 - Bake 20 min. 350° Cool.
Topping frosting - cut cake in 3"
2 cups powd Sugar
1 tbls, ole (optional)
1 tsp vanilla
2 tbls milk -

Here's what's cookin': *Pumpkin Cake Bars*

Recipe from the kitchen of: _____ Serves: _____

4 eggs   2 cups pumpkin (can)

1½ cup sugar. ½ teas salt

1 teas ginger - cinnamon

½ teas cloves   ½ cup oleo melted

1 yellow cake mix

1 cup pecans

13 X 9 X 2 =

Mix top 7 ingred. pour in pan.
Sprinkle dry cake mix on top. Drizzle
Butter over mix - Spread nuts over all. 325° 1hr
20min.
cover with foil loosely to keep from
browning too soon for the 1st half of only
Cut into squares - Serve topped with
whip cream

~ *Do we ever tell our kids the pain and hurt she must have felt when she had to watch her son go through losing his own son, her grandchild when she was 65 in 1984?*

135

Lemon Bread —

1 - Lemon cake mix. *no pudding*
1 pkg. Instant lemon pudding
4 eggs
1 cup water   2½ tbls. poppy
⅓ cup oil.   seed.
        350° - 40 - 50 min.
I make in 5 foil pans - grease/flour.
After done - dump on wax paper
till cool. turning from side to side
once in a while. Wash & rewash &
reuse the pans over & over —
    Mix all the Ingredients to-
gether,

~ *Do we ever tell our kids what it must have like for Grandma Blanche at age 48 to lose her son, Tom, age of 21, in a horrific car accident in 1977?*

~ *Do we ever put ourselves in her shoes and wonder about the agony and pain that she went through alone with no husband to hold her up as she grieved the loss of her own child?*

After her husband's death, Blanche raised her 9 children on her own, always looking for tasty recipes she could make quickly to feed her children and any friends who happened to be around.

During this time, she was employed by Super Valu, the Sunwood Inn and McCullum Plumbing in Morris.

Apple Coffee Bars —

2 eggs
1 cup sugar
1 cup flour.
2 cups raw apples. chopped fine.
1½ teas. baking powder.
Beat eggs & sugar together until
lite. add flour - chopped apples & baking
powder. Dough will be thick. spread
in greased 9 X 13 pan.   (over)

Topping
⅔ c Br. Sugar   6 tbls. butter.
⅔ cup flour — 1 tsp. cinnamon —
Make a crumbly mixture of all Ingred.
using a pastry blender - Put over
top of batter & bake at 300°
                    for 45 min,

🌱 136

Lemon Bars –

9 X 13 Ungreased

1 – Yellow cake mix
        1/3 cup oil – 1 egg
Mix together – will be crumbly.
Bake all but about 1 cup. Pat well –
15 min – in oven. While this is
Baking: Make – 1 – 8oz pkg cream
cheese – 1/3 cup sugar – 1 egg.
1 Teas real lemon juice – Pour
over cooked layer & then crumbly (over)

on top. Bake another 15 min –
Cool & cut into bars –

Walnut Bars – 9 X 13 – 350° 45min
  1 1/2 cup Br. Sugar
3/4 cup flour
    1/4 tsp. salt
2/3 cup cut up walnuts
  3 eggs – 1 1/2 Teas vanilla

Beat eggs well & then all the rest.

Put in well greased pan & cut while
            (over)   warm
roll in powdered sugar & place
on plate –

Blanche's Slush Drinks

Mom loved watching sporting events and was particularly enamoured with Rafael Nadal.

Slush -
    8 cups hot water
    1½ cups Sugar - dissolve
After cool add 2 - 6 oz lemonade
                2 - 6 oz orange juice
Stir in freezer - Ice cream bucket
    2 cups vodka - add with juice
Or no booze - Just slush - add
⅓ cup 7 Up to plain or booze in
glass -

Pina Colada Slush

1 lge. can pineapple juice
1 - 12 oz - frozen lemonade
1 Bottle Pina Colada
1 cup light Booze.

Stir all together in ice
cream pail & freeze. Add 7up. when served.

~ *Do we tell our kids about Grandma Blanche washing load after load of clothes on Saturday morning on an old Maytag wringer washer and hauling them up the steps and outside to hang on the line?*

Orange Lemon Slush.
2 - cups vodka

8 cups hot water - let cool
add 1½ cups sugar - dissolve
after cool add lemon & orange
frozen juice - 12 oz of each -
over
Freeze & Stir occasionally

In glass - add.
⅔ - Slush - ⅓ 7-Up

Punch —

1 pkg Rasberry Kool aid —
1 1/4 c Sugar —
1 frozen can pink Lemonade
8 cups water
1 qt — ginger ale —

Rhubarb Flo. Slush

8-10 cups rhubarb — cut up — cover
with water & cook 10 min. Drain
to 10 cups juice — add 3 cups sugar
3 6 oz cans frozen lemonade. Freeze.
when serving fill glass 2/3 full frozen
slush. fill with 7 up —

~ *Do we ever tell our kids how she walked to church every Sunday in winter and summer, spring and fall and didn't complain because she is a good Catholic woman and feels the need to go to church. And, of course, she didn't want to bother anyone for a ride?*

Russian Tea

3/4 cup Sugar —	1 1/2 cup Sugar
1 cup tang	2 cups tang
1/4 cup Instant Tea	1/2 cup Inst Tea
1/2 teas — Cinnamon	1 teas cinnamon
1/4 tsp. gr. cloves —	1/2 teas cloves

2 heaping tsp. to 1 cup of water

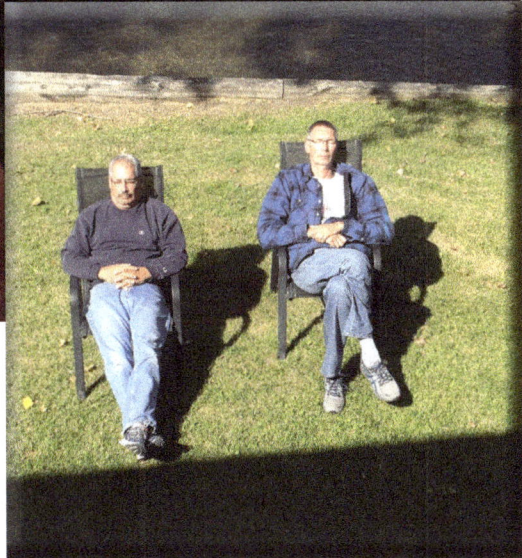

Blanche's
Delicious Miscellaneous

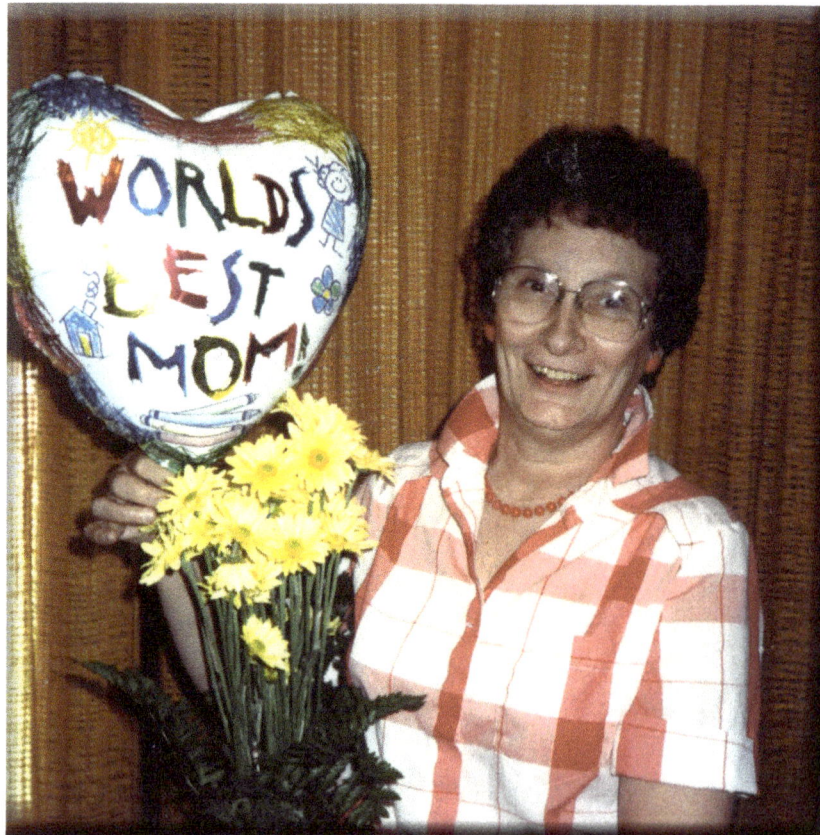

Paper Bag Caramel Pop Corn

Pop about 3/4 C pop corn -
Put on newspaper to get all old maids
out. Let set. I measure about 4 or 5
qts of the pop corn - Put 1/2 in paper bag -

Then boil - 1 c Br Sugar 1 stick ole -
1/4 c white syrup - 1/2 teas. salt.
Stir all the time - Boil 1 1/2 min. take
off add 1/2 teas. soda. Stir 1 Stir

Pour 1/2 over pop corn in bag - Then
add rest of pop corn. Pour remaini.
ingred - Roll top down put in Micro
1 1/2 min. take out shake - put back in
Micro for another 1 1/2 min. take it d
put in clean gro bag. Shake every so
so often till it cools & don't stick
together. I keep in 5 qt. pail.
Keep covered.

Bernice Munchy Treat

1 cup Br. Sugar
¼ cup white syrup   } Micro
1 Stick ole   2 min -

Pour over in sack-
12 oz - crispix   } Micro
½ bag pretzels   1½ min,

Cool - Shake a couple times -
Add nuts & M & M's -

Keep Covered -

Hot Mexican Bean Dip

1 lb. hamb -
½ cup chopped onion,
2 pkge Taco Seasoning
2 cup water
1 can refried beans
1 regular - 1 mild Mexican cheese
1½ cup picante sauce
Mix together in crock - pot on low
until cheese's melted & flavors

Here's what's cookin':
Hidden Valley Ranch -
Recipe from the kitchen of: oyster crackers

Serves:

½ tsp dill weed

¼ lemon pepper

¾ cup Salad oil

¼ tsp. garlic powder -

1 pkge Hidden Valley Ranch Milk Recipe Orig. Ranch Salad Dressing Mix

1 2-16 oz plain oyster crackers.

Whisk together the 1st. five ingred.
Pour over crackers, stirring to coat.
Place on Baking sheets + bake 275°.

for 15-20 mins

Makes 11-12 cups -

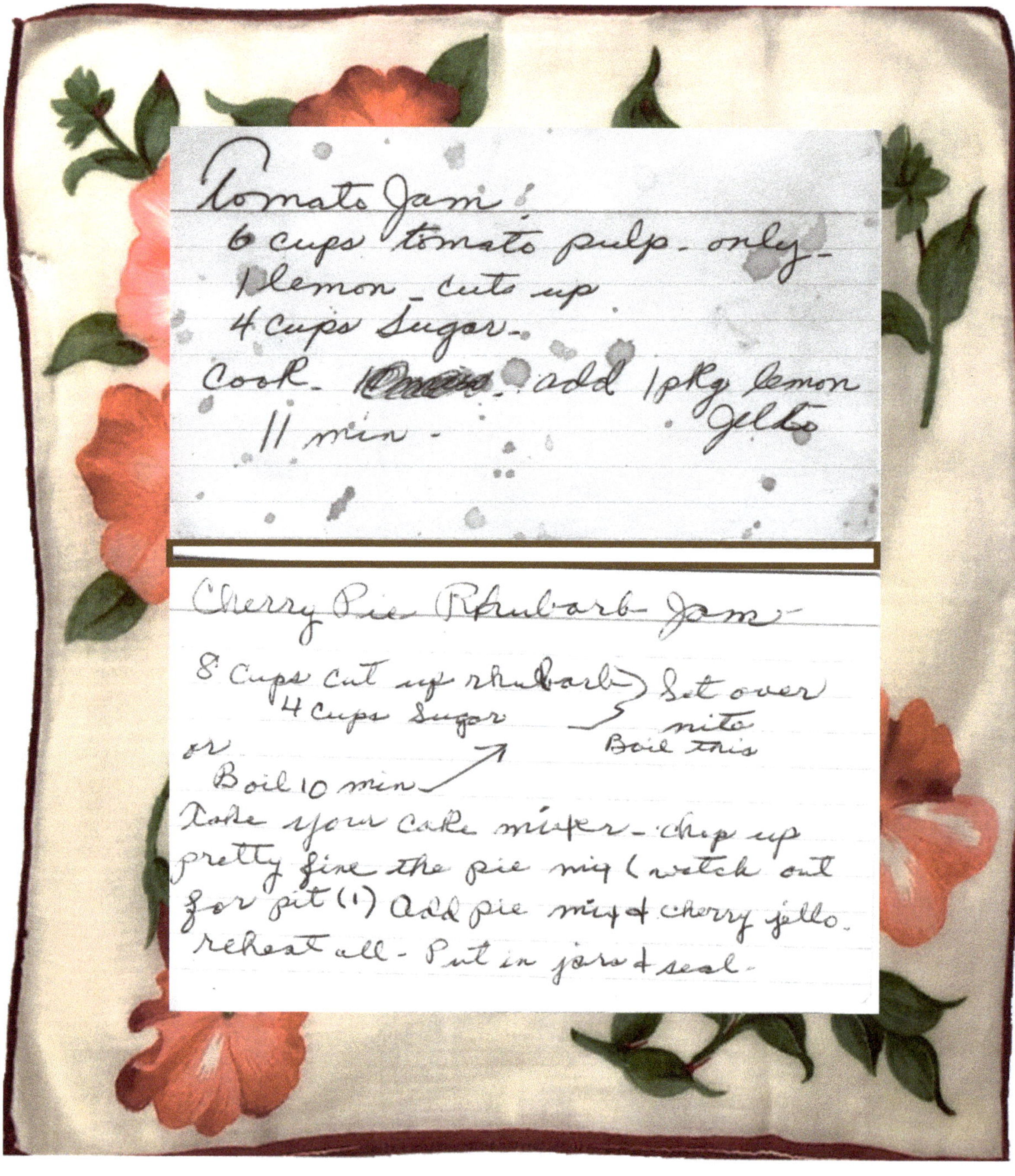

Tomato Jam:
6 cups tomato pulp - only -
1 lemon - cuts up
4 cups Sugar -
Cook - ~~Press~~ add 1 pkg lemon
11 min - Jello

Cherry Pie Rhubarb - Jam -

8 cups cut up rhubarb ⎫ Set over
     4 cups Sugar   ⎬ nite
or   ⎭ Boil this
   Boil 10 min
Take your cake mixer - chop up
pretty fine the pie mix (watch out
for pit (1) Add pie mix & cherry jello.
reheat all - Put in jars & seal -

Tomato Jam.   Bernice's —

3 1/2 cups smashed tomato
Bail 10 min
Skim off water –
add 2 cups sugar Bail 10 min
add 1 lemon jello
   1/2 thin sliced lemon

Rhubarb Cherry Jam –

   8 cups rhubarb – chopped
      4 cups sugar   mix
   Soak over nite or 4–5 hrs, in the
day time –
Bail for 10 min – then add ground
up cherry pie filling & stir well –
Bring to bail add cherry jello 2 3/4 g
                      over

Can also do with
   peach pie + peach jello
or Strawberry pie mix
+ Strawberry jello

Whole Tomatoes _ Wash tomatoes _
_ Wash jars _ let set in sink with
water in. Put one Kettle of hot
water on stove heat to boiling take
off _ Drop a lot of tomatoes in water _
_ Stab with Knife to see if skin
is ready to take off _ Plus the core _
½ tea salt in jar. Cut tomatoes
up & squish in jar _ too : Put
more tomatoes in hot water Then
also remove & peel skin again.

Put boiling lids on & boil in the
Canner for 20 min. of boiling.
I push in jar with hand.
Always wash & wipe the screw
part good & you can use for yes.

~ Do we ever tell our kids how she planted a garden, weeded it and picked the vegetables, then cleaned and canned and canned some more every kind of vegetable and also apples, pears, and peaches so we would have food in the winter?

Tomato Juice –
Wash/put hot water in jars & let stand – Git lids ready in water to boil – Wash tomatoes – cut – in all directions – put in about 3 Rettles & squish with hands. Then ‾‾ t on stove 4 (medium) wash & stir ‾‾ use pancake spatula so they don't burn. Then run thru the sieve. Put juice back in Rettles & heat. Dump out water – 1 tess. salt in each quart – ‾‾ – Whip off rim of jar. Screw on lite. Put in canner under water – Boil 20 min take out & let cool B/4 removing the screw tops.

In 1988, Blanche sold her home at 7 Pine and moved to Bankards Apartments, where she lived for 24 years. She then moved to Heritage Apartments. The little gray home on Pine remained empty long enough for Steve to go back and take pictures of the interior. These are the shelves in the basement that once were stocked with all Blanche's canned goods. From them, she could whip together many of the recipes in this book.

Norwegian Pizza

1st layer - on a pizza pan.

1 2 oz Philie cream cheese

2 tbls lemon juice - 2 tbls. mayo

1/4 c grated onion.   1/4 tsp. garlic?

Mix together & spread on platter -

2nd layer. - 1 Bottle chili sauce

3rd layer - 1 sm can or bag frozen shrimp

& drain & wash - Dry on paper towel,

Put on top -

~ Do we ever tell our kids how proud
we are to have our mom for a mom,
because she set such a wonderful
example for us?

~ Do we notice how she beams when
she has her children in church be-
side her and how proud she must
feel, knowing that her husband is
proud of her too?

~ Do we ever tell our kids how proud
she is of her own children and how
she feels that they are liked because they are kind and gracious
to everyone?

Raw Cuke Slices

6 cups cukes - cut thin - don't remove skins

1/2 cup onions

1 pepper green. chopped

1 1/2 c sugar

1 c vinegar   Pour over all -

1 tbls. salt   keep refrig -

Dill Pickles - Lillies

2 qts water - boil   dill - 1 head

1 qt vinegar brown   in bottom & 1 top

1 c salt - coarse pickling

garlic -   salt

Tiny clove of garlic.

Pickled Beets - Cut off tops to
about 1" left on - fill sink with
water & soak & wash - rinse. Put
big ones together & smaller ones.
Keep clean jars full of hot water till
used. Fill sink with cold water - CK.
beets about 45 min - poke knife thru.
~~Rinse~~ While beets are boiling.
Make this:
2 cups sugar - 2C water - 2C vinegar

Recipe:
From: 1 Teas all Spice   Makes:
1 tablespoon cinnamon - 1 teas cloves.
1/2 teas salt. Boil this & diced beets &
boil 5-8 min. Put in jars & seal.
you can keep the juice for a few days
in jar in frig.
Stir the juice off & on (& use spatula)
Then add beets. Mite turn stove down
a little bit. After in jar - need NO
boiling - Leave screws on.

Bolony Sandwich Spread.

1 ring Bolony. grind -
about 4. eggs or 3 diced
4 sweet pickles .
1/4 or little less pickle juice - 1 cu
1 tbls. onion - chopped -
Then Salad dressing - mayonaise

Corn Bread Pudding

1 can corn (drain)
1 can cream corn
1 stick butter - (melted)
2 eggs
8 oz sour cream
1 Box jiffy corn bread mix
Bake @ 350° - 35-45 min in
ungreased pan uncovered

Scalloped Potatoes -

2 - tables flour
1 1/4 c. milk
1 garlic
1 cup ole
1/4 teas - salt
1/2 c shredded cheese
4 thin onion slices
2 med potatoes

- 20 min -
put & then
flour mixture

Easy Cheesie Potatoes

1 pkge hash potatoes - 2 lb. potatoes
1 1/2 pts (3 cups) 1/2 & 1/2 - cream,

1 1/2 cups. grated Am. or cheddar
1 small onion & ct & pepper -
Layer in greased 9 x 13. Pour half & half
over all & at 350° for 1 1/2 - or 1 hr,
lass pen at 300 to 325°

The Holy Bible

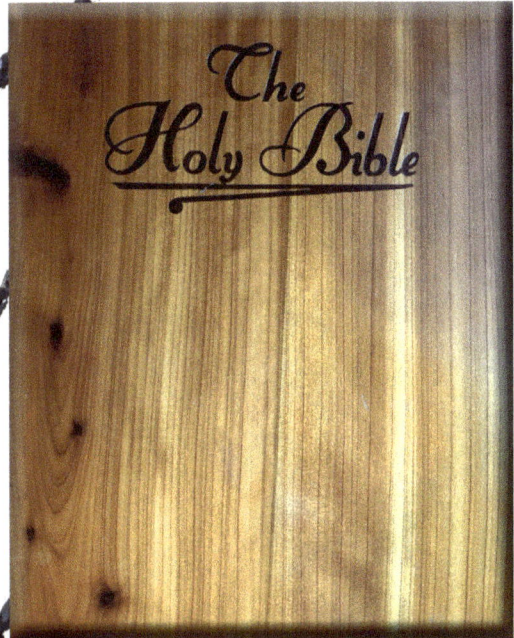

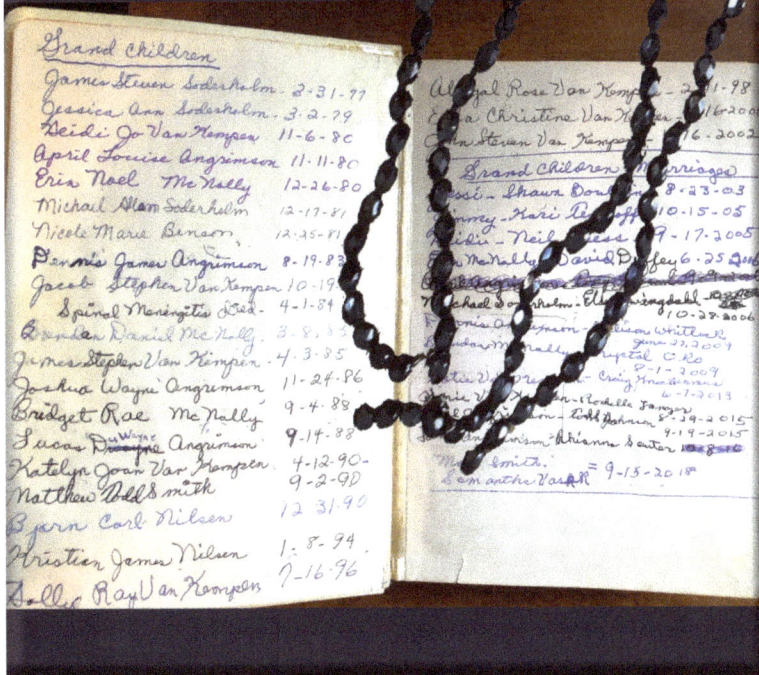

After Blanche retired, she was more involved with church activities. She served on the Altar Guild and was a part of the Prayer Chain.

She volunteered for many years at the Stevens County Historical Museum, West Wind Village, and the Blood Mobile until she was 89 years young. She was a member of the VFW Ladies Auxiliary for over 50 years.

Christmases

159 🌱

~ And do we ever tell our kids how Grandma loved to have fun, how she laughed and enjoyed life to the fullest?

Mom loved putting puzzles together and also would gladly challenge anyone to a game of cribbage. Her lifelong commitment to her family never wavered and throughout her adult life she loved watching her children and grandchildren play in sports. Her favorite professional teams are both from Minnesota—the Twins and the Timberwolves.

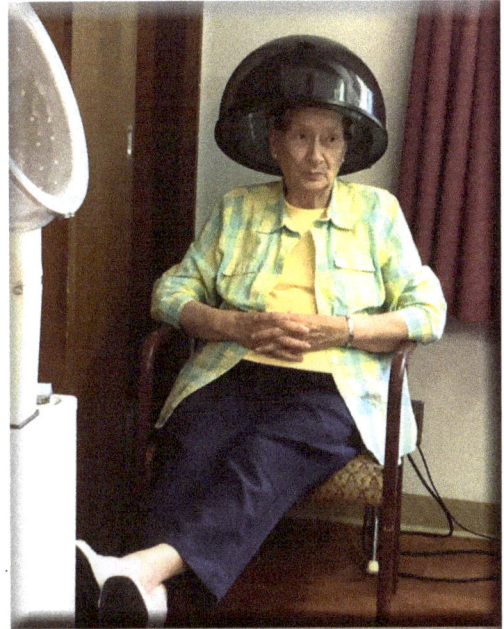

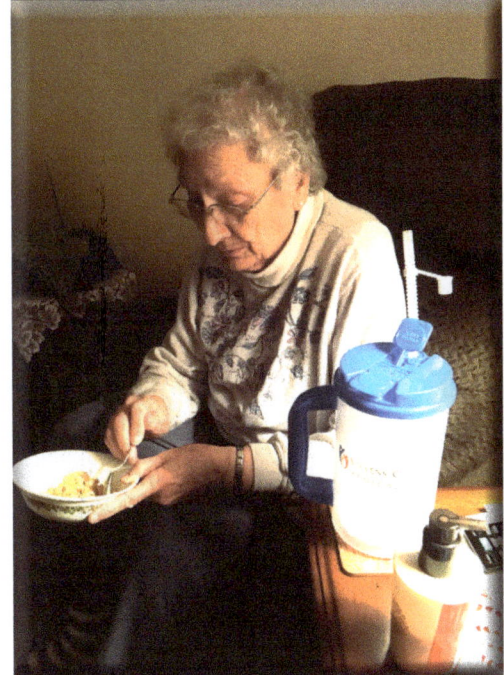

Blanche's Life in her Own Words

Don't Know how to start
this Mary - but here goes.
Our first secret is, I was
born on a farm by Canby
Mn. on Sept. 20, 1928.
Sometime before I was
3 I went into convulsions
& almost died. My mother
died when I was only
1½ yrs. old. We lived on
a farm 10 miles out of
Canby till 1937 & then
we moved to Morris on a
farm - Went to country
school. Had 3 people in
the same grade with me.
We had to walk a mile

to school every day. Then when I started the Freshman year of school we caught a bus to Morris. After I graduated I moved to a room with my sister Madelyn. Got a job working as a dental assistant for 3 dentists. Knew of the Van Kempen's big family in that huge house on main street. Our room that we rented was a block from Florence

2

so I'd baby sit for her
or just go over their a
lot. Washed clothes their
too. In those days, we
just rented rooms for
sleeping & ate all our
meals down town.
Actually met dad in 48.
Our first date was to
the Minnesota State Fair.
Got engaged Feb. 9th of
1950 - and married in
Sept. 14, 1950. Lived in
one of Roy Tucker's apts. on
west side. In Jan. of

3

165 🌿

51 Dad had to go to Memphis Naval Reserve Hospital. I stayd in Morris & kept working at the dentists. Then on March 8th Roebuck drove Irene Van & I down to pick up Jim and went on to Alabama to see Nemo and Nick. I remember I was 5 months pregnant and we had traveled 2300 miles.

We lived in a little apt. in Memphis. Jim

Drove 20 miles to the hospital every day. He had the duty every 3rd weekend & of course I went into labor that weekend. He had to come rushing home to get me & take me back. Vicki was born at 1:20 in the Memphis Navy Hospital. I hated that - It was a huge huge room with lotza woman in labor & having babies. Just like cattle in a barn - Jim kept coming back to check & see if I'd had it. She was my only southern

5

bell. We were pretty happy with our 8 lb. 10 oz. July 4th baby. Got out of service in the summer of 52. We moved into a Navy apt. in the fall. Vicki was about 6 weeks old. Sis had come down to take care of her while I was going to have my goiter removed - (all was free when you were in service) so I was going to get it done B/4 we came home. I'll never forget it! The Drs. gave me an exam like I was a guinea pig. Had about 4 interns looking at me before surgery, Then the last ques, the Dr, asked was when did you have your last period, I told him I was 2 wks, over, He got as white as a sheet, He said, he could of caused a miscarriage with all the exam stuff. Well, that nite I had it !! Sis was staying with us then, So I didn't have my operation at all while Sis was their.

We moved in with Grandma Van for a while. Vicke got a lot of attention. Hurlie was still living at home.

We moved into an up-
stairs apt. Jim was working
for Soker's Construction Co.
Steve & Judy were born
while we lived up their.
I'd lost a baby between
Judy & Tom. We bought our
house in 55. In 56 - Bob
Guter called Jim & asked if he
would like a job at the P.O.
year around. So he grabbed
it. When he'd have vacation
we could never afford to go
away - so Jim would go out
to Soker's & drive a cat & do
road work. He really enjoyed
that. Proceeded to have 5
more darling children.

8

170

Don't know how we did it.
Jim was a great dad. He'd
come home about 2:30 & help.
Dad a nice garden - that he'd
spend many hrs. in. I went
to work at a night club at
5 - 1 about 3 or 4 nites a
week. Once in a while on
Sunday. Then Jim would
make meals. Then when John
started school I went to
work at Super Valu as a
checker. Worked their till
Jim got sick with cancer.
He had been doctoring for
a year for an ulcer & finally
he asked the Dr. if he
could get a second opinion.
9

171

The ulcer just didn't seem to be getting better and the Dr. wanted him to go see a psychiatrist. So we headed for Mpls – for exploratory. Porky & I had sat outside his room during surgery & were playing cribbage. The Drs. had told us we should go home as the surgery would take 2 to 3 hrs. Just thought they'd remove the ulcer. Never forget that May 2nd, 1969 day. 15 min. after Jim went into surgery my name was called & the Dr. was as cool as cool could be & said - "Your

husband is full of cancer
& has 4 months to live!
Flo, Ber, Spike's-Nick's & Sis
were just great. Taking care
of all you kids. Course you
kids had stories to tell
about the homes. We stayed
in the cities for about 1½ wks.
I learned to give shots, Pretty
scarey. Jim was such a good
patient. Dr. had told us to
keep him as quiet as he
needed. I couldn't believe
what I'd do with 9 kids.
I wished I'd written a log
book. Sis was great. Dad
come to stay with us
off & on. Had some fun

11

times with Jim. He just couldn't understand how God could deal us sucha blow - 9 kids - 18 - 4. Did drive himself to the clinic once in a while. I remember at first he was pretty good & would do stuff. I'd find him in the garden at 5 AM pulling weeds. They gave him the drug called dilaudid. Never had chemo. Jeepers, I can't even write this & I'm crying. Mary!! I hope none of you kids ever have to watch a husband die that way. It was hard on you kids. Being dished out

174

& come home & go again. When I think back of how everybody would take you guys — whether they had plans or not. Even having their families to raise besides. Jim could never stand noise. you guys would try to be good & shut the door so quietly & hed still hear it. Jim had 2 months vacation coming & about 4 months sick leave, So his pay check kept coming in. I quit work. I remember I went to work one day & was home before noon. I

13

just worried so bad. Bob Guter was so nice (Jim's boss). Did bring bananas & have $20 stuck in it. His post-office buddies were good to come see him. He died on Sept. 5th, 1969. It was a blessed day really, I knew he was trying to hide his pain, toward the end.

He was happy to have seen Vicki graduate from school, at least. Steve was a junior. I don't think John quite understood it. He was home for a year after Jim died & that was

14

good for me. Life does go on. I was always thankful I had all you kids to keep me busy. Was very hard at times. Loved each & every one of you, Then after graduations the marriages started. Then the grand kids. Then on July 29, 1977. Tom, my 4th in line got killed in a car accident. I think I was numb for months. I remember the Dr. gave me pills to get sleep. So, I was nuts. Lost my glasses. Forgot where I'd put them & had left them at the beauty

15

177

shop. In 1988 I sold our house and moved to an apt. So far I've got 7 married - 1 divorced - 16 grandchildren. Get to go see them every once in a while. Never had a car all these years.

16

1963

1970

"To Life"
2019

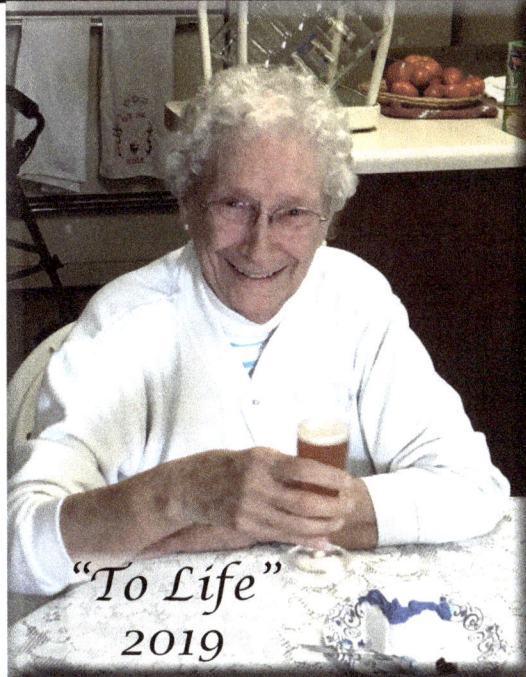

Love you all
Mom

Blanche's Treasured Descendants

Epilogue

On her 91st Birthday, Blanche's children presented her with this token of their love for her. Her surprise was matched only by her joy in seeing what her children had created.

Many adults struggle to find ways to thank their mothers for giving them life, for demonstrating how to navigate life's difficult times, and for being, in old age, a joyful, grateful human being, someone whose love still warms your heart and whose spirit you want to emulate.

Creator, Mary Van Kempen Nilsen, came up with one way: preserve her recipes—not just the recipes, but the actual well-worn cards on which they were written, cards that were, in some cases yellowed with age and spotted with a stray ingredient.

Her brothers and sisters agreed. And as the energy built, so did the scope of the project. Not just recipes (a metaphor for all that their mother gives them that nourishes their lives), but old pictures too. Not just recipes and pictures but their mother's own words about her life. Not just recipes and pictures and writing, but a tribute to the man she loved, the man who died much too soon.

This book is the result, a way the children of Blanche Van Kempen found to say to their mother, now a ninety-one-year-old, grace-filled matriarch, "Mom, thank you!" "Mom, we love you."

www.ingramcontent.com/pod-product-compliance
Lightning Source LLC
Chambersburg PA
CBHW060751150426
42811CB00058B/1379